home
food

home
food

MURDOCH BOOKS

Contents

Breakfast

Scrambled eggs and salmon on brioche

4 fresh eggs
4 tablespoons cream
2 tablespoons unsalted butter
125 g (4½ oz) smoked salmon, sliced
2 teaspoons finely chopped dill
2 individual brioche buns or
  2 croissants

Crack the eggs into a bowl, add the cream and beat well together. Season with some salt and freshly ground black pepper.

Melt the butter in a non-stick frying pan. When it starts to sizzle, add the eggs and turn the heat down to low. Using a flat-ended wooden spoon, push the mixture around until it starts to set, then add the salmon and dill. Continue to cook, gently folding the salmon and dill through the mixture until the eggs are mostly cooked, and just a little liquid left in the pan.

Cut the top off the brioche or croissants, scoop out some of the filling, then pile the scrambled eggs on top and serve.

Serves 2

Savoury breakfast tarts

220 g (1¾ cups) plain
   (all-purpose) flour
140 g (5 oz) butter, diced
9 eggs
4 slices ham
2 tablespoons chopped parsley
2 medium tomatoes, finely chopped
125 ml (½ cup) cream
4 tablespoons grated Parmesan
   cheese

Preheat the oven to 200°C (400°F/ Gas 6). Sift the flour and ½ teaspoon of salt into a food processor, add the butter and process for a few seconds until the mixture resembles breadcrumbs. Bring the dough together using your hands and shape into a ball. Wrap the ball in plastic wrap, flatten slightly, and put in the fridge for 10 minutes.

Roll the pastry out on a floured work surface until it is very thin. Cut out four 16 cm (6½ in) circles and use them to line four 10 cm (4 in) tartlet tins. Press the pastry gently into the flutes of the tins. Line each tin with a piece of crumpled greaseproof paper and some uncooked rice. Bake the pastry for 5 minutes, then take out the paper and rice and bake for another minute.

Line each pastry base with the ham (you may need to cut it into pieces to make it fit neatly). Sprinkle with the parsley and add the tomato. Gently break two eggs into each tin, then pour a quarter of the cream over the top of each, sprinkle with Parmesan and dust with salt and pepper.

Put the tarts in the oven and bake for 10–12 minutes, or until the egg whites are set. Serve hot or cold.

Serves 4

Cheese and onion waffles with herbed ricotta and roast tomato

4 Roma (plum) tomatoes, halved
1 tablespoon olive oil
1 tablespoon balsamic vinegar
1 teaspoon sugar
1 tablespoon chopped oregano
310 g (1¼ cups) low-fat ricotta
    cheese
4 tablespoons chopped herbs
    (oregano, sage, rosemary, parsley)
185 g (1½ cups) self-raising flour
3 tablespoons freshly grated
    Parmesan cheese
3 tablespoons grated low-fat
    Cheddar cheese
3 large spring onions (scallions),
    finely chopped
1 egg
250 ml (1 cup) low-fat milk
2 egg whites
fresh oregano sprigs, to garnish

Preheat the oven to 160°C (315°F/ Gas 2–3). Lightly grease an oven tray. Place the tomato halves on the tray and drizzle the cut surface with olive oil and balsamic vinegar. Sprinkle with the sugar, oregano and salt. Bake for 1 hour, or until very soft. Put the ricotta in a bowl and fold in the chopped herbs. Season to taste. Divide the herbed ricotta mixture into 4 even portions. Refrigerate until needed.

Meanwhile, place the flour, Parmesan, Cheddar, spring onion, whole egg and milk in a bowl. Season with salt and black pepper, then mix well. Whisk the egg whites until soft peaks form and gently fold into the cheese and egg mixture.

Preheat a waffle iron and brush lightly with olive oil. Pour in 80 ml (⅓ cup) waffle batter and cook until golden on both sides. Keep warm in the oven while you cook the remaining waffles.

To serve, arrange the waffle halves on each serving plate with two tomato halves and some herbed ricotta mixture on the side. Garnish with a sprig of fresh oregano.

Serves 4

French toast with crispy prosciutto

3 tablespoons thickened cream
  or milk
3 eggs
3 tablespoons caster (superfine) sugar
pinch of cinnamon
about 80 g (1/3 cup) butter
8 thick slices bread, cut in half
  diagonally
1 tablespoon olive oil
12 slices prosciutto

Put the cream, eggs, sugar and cinnamon in a wide, shallow bowl and mix together. Soak the bread in the egg mixture, one slice at a time, shaking off any excess.

Melt half the butter in a frying pan. When it is sizzling, add 3–4 slices of bread in a single layer and cook until golden brown on both sides. Cook the remaining bread in batches, adding more butter as needed, and keeping the cooked slices warm in the oven until all are done.

Next, in a separate frying pan, heat the olive oil. When hot, add the prosciutto and fry until crisp. Remove and drain on paper towels. Place the prosciutto on top of the French toast and serve.

Serves 4

Fried eggs and tomatoes on spring onion potato cakes

Spring onion potato cakes

300 g (10½ oz) potatoes, peeled and roughly chopped
1 egg yolk
50 g (¾ oz) grated Cheddar cheese
3 spring onions (scallions), trimmed and finely chopped
2 tablespoons finely chopped flat-leaf (Italian) parsley
1 tablespoon plain (all-purpose) flour
2 tablespoons olive oil

2 tablespoons olive oil
1 garlic clove, sliced
3 Roma (plum) tomatoes, halved lengthways
butter, for frying
4 eggs

Boil the potatoes in a saucepan of salted water until tender. Drain, then return the potatoes to the pan over low heat to evaporate off any moisture. Remove the pan from the heat and mash the potatoes. Stir in the egg yolk, cheese, spring onions and parsley and season. Form into 4 patty shapes. Tip the flour onto a plate and lightly coat the patties with it. Cover and chill for 30 minutes.

Heat the olive oil in a large frying pan over medium heat. Fry the patties for 4–5 minutes on both sides until golden brown. Keep warm until needed.

In a separate frying pan, cook the garlic and tomatoes. Heat the olive oil in the pan over low heat. Add the garlic and fry for 2 minutes. Add the tomatoes cut-side down and fry for 10–15 minutes, turning them once during cooking.

Heat a heavy-based non-stick frying pan over medium heat and add 2 tablespoons oil and a little butter. When the butter is sizzling, break the eggs into the frying pan and fry. Cook for about 1 minute. Turn off the heat and leave to stand for 1 minute. Serve the eggs with the spring onion potato cakes and tomatoes.

Serves 2

Eggs benedict

12 eggs, straight from the fridge
8 slices prosciutto
4 English muffins, split
200 g (7 oz) butter
2 tablespoons lemon juice

Turn on the grill (broiler). Put a large frying pan full of water over high heat. When the water is bubbling, turn the heat down to a simmer. Crack an egg into a cup and slip the egg into the water. The egg should start to turn opaque as it hits the water. Do the same with 7 more eggs, keeping them separated. Turn the heat down and leave the eggs for 3 minutes.

Put the prosciutto on a baking tray, place it under the grill for 2 minutes, then turn it over and cook the other side. Put the muffins in a toaster or under the grill to toast.

Crack the remaining 4 eggs into a blender, put the lid on and leave the top hole open. Heat the butter in a small pan, until it has melted.

Start the blender and pour in the butter in a steady stream through the top hole. The eggs should thicken straight away to make a thick sauce. Add the lemon juice and season the hollandaise with salt and black pepper.

Put the muffins on plates and put a slice of prosciutto on each. Lift each egg out of the water, drain and put them on top of the prosciutto. Spoon some hollandaise over each egg.

Serves 4

Grilled field mushrooms with garlic and chilli

4 large or 8 medium field mushrooms
2 tablespoons butter, softened
1 garlic clove, crushed
1–2 small red chillies, finely chopped
4 tablespoons finely chopped parsley
4 thick slices ciabatta
tomato chutney or relish
crème fraîche, to serve

Put the grill (broiler) on and cover the grill rack with a piece of foil so any juices stay with the mushrooms as they cook. Gently pull the stalks out of the mushrooms and peel off the skins.

Mix together the butter, garlic, chilli and parsley and spread some over the inside of each mushroom. Make sure the butter is quite soft so it spreads easily. Season well.

Grill the mushrooms under a medium heat for about 8 minutes — they need to be cooked right through. Test the centres with the point of a knife if you are not sure.

Toast the bread, spread some tomato chutney or relish on each slice, then top with a mushroom (or two) and serve straight away. Serve with a dollop of crème fraîche.

Serves 4

Piperade

2 tablespoons olive oil
1 large onion, thinly sliced
2 red capsicums (peppers), seeded
  and cut into batons
2 garlic cloves, crushed
750 g (1 lb 10 oz) tomatoes
pinch of cayenne pepper
8 eggs, lightly beaten
1 tablespoon butter
4 thin slices of ham, such as Bayonne

Heat the oil in a large, heavy-based frying pan over medium heat, then add the onion. Cook for about 3 minutes, or until soft. Add the capsicum and garlic, cover and cook for 8 minutes, stirring frequently to ensure the mixture doesn't brown.

Score a cross in the base of each tomato. Put in a large bowl of boiling water for 20 seconds, then drain and plunge into a bowl of cold water. Remove the tomatoes and peel the skin away from the cross. Chop the flesh and discard the cores. Add the chopped tomato and cayenne to the capsicum mixture, cover the pan and cook for a further 5 minutes.

Uncover the pan and increase the heat. Cook for 3 minutes, or until the juices have evaporated, shaking the pan often. Season well with salt and freshly ground black pepper. Add the eggs and scramble into the mixture until fully cooked.

Heat the butter in a small frying pan over medium heat and fry the ham. Arrange the piperade on four plates, top with the cooked ham and serve with buttered toast.

Serves 4

Mushroom omelette with chorizo

50 g (1³/₄ oz) butter
1 medium chorizo sausage, sliced
100 g (3¹/₂ oz) mushrooms, finely
 sliced
6 eggs
2 tablespoons chives, finely chopped

Heat 30 g (1 oz) of the butter in a small omelette pan or frying pan over medium heat. Add the chorizo and fry for about 5 minutes, or until golden. Remove from the pan using a slotted spoon. Add the mushrooms to the pan and cook, stirring frequently, for about 4 minutes, or until soft. Add to the chorizo.

Break the eggs into a bowl and season with salt and freshly ground black pepper. Add the chives and beat lightly with a fork.

Put half the remaining butter in the pan and melt over medium heat until foaming. Add half the eggs and cook for 20 seconds, in which time they will start to set on the bottom, then quickly stir the mixture with a fork. Work quickly, drawing away some of the cooked egg from the bottom of the pan and allowing some of the uncooked egg to set, tilting the pan a little as you go. Once the eggs are mostly set, arrange half the mushrooms and chorizo on top. Cook for 1 minute more, if necessary. Tip the omelette out onto a plate and keep warm while the second omelette is cooking. Repeat with the remaining ingredients. Serve as soon as both omelettes are cooked.

Serves 2

Croque madame

3 eggs
1 tablespoon milk
1½ tablespoons butter, softened
4 slices good-quality white bread
1 teaspoon Dijon mustard
4 slices Gruyère cheese
2 slices leg ham
2 teaspoons vegetable oil

Crack 1 egg into a wide, shallow bowl, add the milk and lightly beat. Season with salt and freshly ground black pepper.

Butter the bread using ½ tablespoon of the butter and spread half the slices with Dijon mustard. Place a slice of cheese on top, then the ham and then another slice of cheese. Top with the remaining bread.

Heat the remaining butter and vegetable oil in a large non-stick frying pan over medium heat. While the butter is melting, dip one sandwich into the egg and milk mixture, coating the bread on both sides. When the butter is sizzling but not brown, add the sandwich and cook for 1½ minutes on one side, pressing down firmly with a spatula. Turn over and cook the other side, then move it to the side of the pan.

Gently break an egg into the pan and fry until it is done to your liking. Transfer the sandwich to a plate and top with the fried egg. Keep warm while you repeat with the remaining sandwich and egg, adding more butter and oil to the pan if necessary. Serve immediately.

Makes 2 sandwiches

Cheese and herb cornbread with scrambled eggs

Cornbread
155 g (1¼ cups) self-raising flour
1 tablespoon caster (superfine) sugar
2 teaspoons baking powder
1 teaspoon salt
110 g (¾ cup) fine polenta
60 g (½ cup) grated Cheddar cheese
30 g (½ cup) chopped mixed herbs
    (chives, dill, parsley)
2 eggs
250 ml (1 cup) buttermilk
80 ml (⅓ cup) macadamia or olive oil

Scrambled eggs
6 eggs
125 ml (½ cup) cream
small basil leaves, to garnish

Preheat the oven to 180°C (350°F/ Gas 4). Grease a 20 x 10 cm (8 x 4 in) loaf tin. Sift the flour, sugar, baking powder and salt into a bowl. Add the polenta, Cheddar, herbs, eggs, buttermilk and oil and mix to combine. Spoon the mixture into the loaf tin and bake for 45 minutes, or until a skewer inserted into the centre comes out clean. Remove from the tin.

To make the scrambled eggs, whisk together the eggs and cream and season with salt and pepper. Pour the mixture into a non-stick frying pan and cook over a low heat, stirring occasionally until the egg is just set. (The more you stir the eggs, the more scrambled they become.) Serve the scrambled eggs with slices of buttered cornbread. Sprinkle with basil leaves.

Serves 4

Huevos rancheros

1 ½ tablespoons olive oil
1 white onion, finely chopped
1 green capsicum (pepper), finely
  chopped
2 red chillies, finely chopped
1 garlic clove, crushed
½ teaspoon dried oregano
2 tomatoes, chopped
2 x 400 g (14 oz) can chopped
  tomatoes
8 eggs
4 flour tortillas
100 g (⅔ cup) feta cheese, crumbled

Put the olive oil in a large frying pan (one with a lid) over a medium heat. Add the onion and green capsicum and fry them gently together for 3 minutes, or until they are soft.

Add the chilli and garlic and stir briefly, then add the oregano, fresh and tinned tomatoes, and 180 ml (¾ cup) water. Bring to the boil, then turn down the heat, cover with a lid and simmer gently for 8–10 minutes, or until the sauce thickens. Season with salt and pepper.

Smooth the surface of the mixture, then make eight hollows with the back of a spoon. Break an egg into each hollow and put the lid on the pan. Cook the eggs for 5 minutes, or until they are set.

While the eggs are cooking, heat the tortillas according to the instructions on the packet and cut each into quarters.

Serve the eggs with some feta crumbled over them and the tortillas on the side.

Serves 4

Banana bread

3 ripe bananas, well mashed
2 eggs, well beaten
2 teaspoons grated orange zest
250 g (2 cups) plain (all-purpose) flour
1 teaspoon ground cinnamon
1 teaspoon salt
1 teaspoon bicarbonate of soda
180 g (3/4 cup) caster (superfine) sugar
75 g (2 1/2 oz) walnuts, coarsely chopped

Preheat the oven to 180ºC (350ºF/ Gas 4). Grease a 17 x 8 cm (7 x 3 in) loaf tin.

Combine the bananas, eggs and orange zest in a large bowl. Sift in the flour, cinnamon, salt and bicarbonate of soda, mix, then add the sugar and walnuts. Mix thoroughly, then tip into the prepared tin. Bake for 1 hour and 10 minutes, or until a skewer inserted into the centre comes out clean.

To serve, eat warm or allow to cool, then toast and serve buttered.

Makes 1 loaf

Creamed rice with minted citrus compote

150 g (³/₄ cup) basmati rice
500 ml (2 cups) milk
4 cardamom pods, bruised
¹/₂ cinnamon stick
1 clove
3 tablespoons honey
1 teaspoon natural vanilla extract

Minted citrus compote
2 ruby grapefruit, peeled and
  segmented
2 oranges, peeled and segmented
3 tablespoons orange juice
1 teaspoon grated lime zest
3 tablespoons honey
8 fresh mint leaves, finely chopped

Cook the rice in a large saucepan of boiling water for 12 minutes, stirring occasionally. Drain and cool.

Place the rice, milk, cardamom pods, cinnamon stick and clove in a saucepan and bring to the boil. Reduce the heat to low and simmer for 15 minutes, stirring occasionally, until the milk is absorbed and the rice is creamy. Remove the spices, then stir in the honey and vanilla.

To make the compote, combine the ruby grapefruit, orange, orange juice, lime zest, honey and mint and mix until the honey has dissolved. Serve with the rice.

Serves 4

Cinnamon porridge with caramel figs and cream

200 g (2 cups) rolled oats
¼ teaspoon ground cinnamon
50 g (1¾ oz) butter
115 g (½ cup) brown sugar
300 ml (10½ fl oz) cream
6 fresh figs, halved
milk, to serve
thick (double/heavy) cream, to serve

Place the oats, 1 litre (4 cups) water and cinnamon in a saucepan and stir over a medium heat for 5 minutes, or until the porridge becomes thick and smooth. Set the porridge aside.

Melt the butter in a large frying pan, add all but 2 tablespoons of the brown sugar and stir until it dissolves. Stir in the cream and bring to the boil, then simmer for 5 minutes, or until the sauce starts to thicken slightly.

Place the figs onto a baking tray, sprinkle with the remaining sugar and grill (broil) until the sugar is melted.

Spoon the porridge into individual bowls, top with a little milk, then divide the figs and the caramel sauce among the bowls. Top each serving with a large dollop of thick cream.

Serves 4

Healthy nut and seed muesli

100 g (3½ oz) puffed corn
150 g (1½ cups) rolled oats
100 g (1 cup) pecans
135 g (1 cup) macadamia nuts,
  roughly chopped
100 g (3½ oz) flaked coconut
200 g (7 oz) LSA (linseed, sunflower
  and almond mix)
100 g (3½ oz) dried apples, chopped
200 g (7 oz) dried apricots, chopped
125 g (4½ oz) dried pears, chopped
125 ml (½ cup) maple syrup
1 teaspoon natural vanilla extract

Preheat the oven to 180°C (350°F/
Gas 4). Place the puffed corn, rolled
oats, pecans, macadamia nuts,
coconut, LSA, apples, apricots and
pears in a bowl and mix to combine.

Place the maple syrup and vanilla in a
small saucepan and cook over a low
heat for 3 minutes, or until the maple
syrup becomes easy to pour. Pour
the maple syrup over the mixture and
toss lightly to coat.

Divide the muesli mixture between
two non-stick baking dishes. Bake for
about 20 minutes, turning frequently,
until the muesli is lightly toasted.
Allow the mixture to cool before
transferring it to an airtight container.

Makes 1 kg (2 lb 4 oz)

Blueberry pancakes

250 ml (1 cup) buttermilk
1 egg, lightly beaten
1 tablespoon melted butter
1 teaspoon natural vanilla extract
115 g (¾ cup) plain (all-purpose) flour
1 teaspoon baking powder
½ teaspoon salt
2 ripe bananas, mashed
100 g (3½ oz) blueberries
1 teaspoon vegetable oil
maple syrup, to serve

Put the buttermilk, egg, butter and vanilla essence in a bowl and whisk together. Sift in the flour, baking powder and salt, then stir, making sure not to over blend as the batter should be lumpy. Add the fruit.

Heat the oil in a frying pan over medium heat. Add 60 ml (¼ cup) of batter to the pan for each pancake. Cook for 3 minutes, or until the pancakes are golden brown on the bottom. Turn over and cook for 1 minute more. Repeat with the rest of the batter, keeping the cooked pancakes warm. Serve immediately, drizzled with maple syrup.

Makes about 12 pancakes

Grilled stone fruits with cinnamon toast

2 tablespoons low-fat margarine
1½ teaspoons ground cinnamon
4 thick slices good-quality brioche
4 ripe plums, halved and stones removed
4 ripe nectarines, halved and stones removed
2 tablespoons warmed blossom honey

Place the margarine and 1 teaspoon of the ground cinnamon in a bowl and mix until well combined. Grill (broil) the brioche on one side until golden. Spread the other side with half the cinnamon spread, then grill until golden. Keep warm in the oven.

Brush the plums and nectarines with the remaining spread and cook under a grill (broiler) or on a ridged grill plate, until the spread is bubbling and the fruit is tinged at the edges.

To serve, place 2 plum halves and 2 nectarine halves on each toasted slice of brioche. Dust with the remaining cinnamon and drizzle with the warmed honey.

Serves 4

Note: Tinned plums or apricots may be used in place of fresh stone fruits.

Raspberry breakfast crepes

250 g (2 cups) plain (all-purpose) flour
pinch of salt
1 teaspoon sugar
2 eggs, lightly beaten
500 ml (2 cups) milk
1 tablespoon melted butter
400 g (3⅓ cups) raspberries
icing (confectioners') sugar, for
    dusting
maple syrup or honey, to serve

Sift the flour, salt and sugar into a bowl and make a well in the centre. In a jug or bowl, mix the eggs and milk together with 100 ml (3½ fl oz) water. Slowly pour the mixture into the well, whisking all the time to incorporate the flour and ensure a smooth batter. Stir in the melted butter. Cover and refrigerate for 20 minutes.

Heat a crepe pan or a small non-stick frying pan over medium heat and lightly grease. Pour in enough batter to coat the base of the pan in a thin, even layer. Tip out any excess. Cook for 1 minute, or until the crepe starts to come away from the side of the pan. Turn over and cook on the other side for 1 minute more until just golden. Repeat the process, stacking the crepes on a plate with greaseproof paper between them and covered with foil, until all the batter is used up.

To serve, put one crepe on a serving plate. Arrange some raspberries on a quarter of the crepe. Fold the crepe in half, then in half again, so that the raspberries are wrapped in a little triangular pocket. Repeat with the remaining crepes and raspberries. Dust with icing sugar, drizzle with maple syrup or honey, and serve.

Makes 8 large crepes

Mixed berry couscous

185 g (1 cup) couscous
500 ml (2 cups) apple and cranberry
  juice
1 cinnamon stick
150 g (5½ oz) raspberries
150 g (5½ oz) blueberries
150 g (5½ oz) blackberries
150 g (5½ oz) strawberries, halved
zest of 1 lime
zest of 1 orange
200 g (7 oz) thick Greek-style yoghurt
2 tablespoons golden syrup
mint leaves, to garnish

Place the couscous in a bowl. Place the apple and cranberry juice in a saucepan with the cinnamon stick. Bring to the boil, then remove from the heat and pour over the couscous. Cover with plastic wrap and allow to stand for 5 minutes, or until all the liquid has been absorbed. Remove and discard the cinnamon stick.

Separate the grains of the couscous with a fork, add the raspberries, blueberries, blackberries, strawberries, lime zest and orange zest and fold through gently. Spoon the mixture into four bowls and serve with a generous dollop of yoghurt and a drizzle of golden syrup. Garnish with mint leaves.

Serves 4

Ginger and ricotta flatcakes with fresh honeycomb

150 g (1 cup) wholemeal flour
2 teaspoons baking powder
2 teaspoons ground ginger
2 tablespoons caster (superfine) sugar
55 g (1 cup) flaked coconut, toasted
4 eggs, separated
500 g (2 cups) ricotta cheese
310 ml (1¼ cups) milk
4 bananas, sliced
200 g (7 oz) fresh honeycomb, broken
    into large pieces

Sift the flour, baking powder, ginger and sugar into a bowl. Stir in the coconut and make a well in the centre. Add the combined egg yolks, 350 g (12 oz) of the ricotta and all of the milk. Mix until smooth.

Beat the egg whites until soft peaks form, then fold into the pancake mixture.

Heat a frying pan over a low heat and brush lightly with a little melted butter or oil. Pour 60 ml (¼ cup) of the batter into the pan and swirl gently to create an even pancake. Cook until bubbles form on the surface. Flip and cook the other side for 1 minute, or until golden. Repeat until all the batter is used up.

Stack three pancakes onto each plate and top with a generous dollop of ricotta, banana and a large piece of fresh honeycomb.

Serves 4

Lunch

Thai chicken sausage rolls

500 g (1 lb 2 oz) minced (ground)
  chicken
1 teaspoon ground cumin
1 teaspoon ground coriander
2 tablespoons sweet chilli sauce
2 tablespoons chopped coriander
  (cilantro) leaves
80 g (1 cup) fresh breadcrumbs
2 sheets frozen puff pastry, thawed
1 egg, lightly beaten
1 tablespoon sesame seeds
baby rocket (arugula) leaves, to serve
sweet chilli sauce, extra, for dipping

Preheat the oven to 200°C (400°F/
Gas 6). Combine the chicken, cumin,
coriander, chilli sauce, coriander
leaves and breadcrumbs in a bowl.

Spread the mixture along one edge
of each pastry sheet and roll up to
conceal the filling. Place the rolls
seam-side down on a tray lined with
baking paper, brush lightly with the
beaten egg and sprinkle with sesame
seeds. Bake for 30 minutes, or until
golden and cooked through. Slice the
rolls and serve with rocket and sweet
chilli sauce.

Serves 6–8

Fattoush with fried haloumi

2 Lebanese (short) cucumbers
4 pitta breads
1 garlic clove, crushed
2 tablespoons lemon juice
5 tablespoons olive oil
4 spring onions (scallions), sliced
4 tomatoes, diced
2 green capsicums (peppers), diced
1 bunch flat-leaf (Italian) parsley,
   chopped
2 tablespoons mint, chopped
2 tablespoons oregano, chopped
sumac, optional
1 kg (2 lb 4 oz) haloumi cheese, cut
   into 8 slices

Turn on the grill (broiler). Peel the cucumber, cut it into quarters lengthways, then cut each piece into thick slices. Put these in a sieve and sprinkle with a little salt to help drain off any excess liquid, which would make the salad soggy.

Split each pitta bread in half and toast them on both sides to make the bread crisp. When the bread is crisp, break it into small pieces. Mix the garlic, lemon juice and 4 tablespoons of the oil to make a dressing. Rinse and drain the cucumber.

Put the cucumber, spring onion, tomato, green capsicum, parsley, mint and oregano in a large bowl. Add the dressing and toss everything together well.

Heat the last tablespoon of oil in a non-stick frying pan and fry the haloumi cheese on both sides until it is browned. Scatter the bread over the salad and fold it through.

Serve the fattoush with the slices of haloumi on top. Sprinkle with a little sumac.

Serves 4

Spanish omelette with smoked salmon

1 tablespoon olive oil
400 g (14 oz) potatoes, peeled
  and cubed
1 onion, finely chopped
8 eggs
2 tablespoons dill, chopped
8 slices smoked salmon
80 g (⅓ cup) mascarpone cheese
4 handfuls salad leaves

Heat the oil in a non-stick frying pan and add the potato cubes. Fry them gently, stirring them so they brown on all sides and cook through to the middle. This should take about 10 minutes. Cut a cube open to see if they are cooked through completely.

When the potato is cooked, add the onion and cook it gently for a few minutes until it is translucent and soft. Switch on the grill (broiler).

When the onion is almost ready, break the eggs into a bowl and whisk them together with some salt and freshly ground pepper and the dill.

Tear the smoked salmon into pieces and add it to the frying pan. Add the mascarpone in blobs. Using a spatula, pull the mixture into the centre of the pan and level it off. Pour the eggs over the top and cook for 5–10 minutes, or until the omelette is just set.

Put the frying pan under the grill for a minute or two to lightly brown the top of the omelette. Slide the omelette out of the frying pan and cut it into eight wedges. Arrange a handful of salad leaves on each plate and top with two wedges of omelette.

Serves 4

Bagels with smoked salmon and caper salsa

4 plain or rye bagels
100 g (3½ oz) neufchatel cream
  cheese
200 g (7 oz) sliced smoked salmon
2 spring onions (scallions), chopped
2 Roma (plum) tomatoes, finely
  chopped
2 tablespoons baby capers
2 tablespoons finely chopped
  fresh dill
2 tablespoons lemon juice
1 tablespoon extra virgin olive oil

Cut the bagels in half and spread the base generously with cream cheese, then top with the salmon.

Combine the spring onion, tomato, capers, dill, lemon juice and olive oil in a bowl. Pile this mixture onto the salmon and serve.

Serves 4

Wild rice salad

95 g (¹/₂ cup) wild rice
250 ml (1 cup) chicken stock
1 tablespoon butter
100 g (¹/₂ cup) basmati rice
2 rashers bacon, rind removed,
   chopped and cooked
110 g (³/₄ cup) currants
60 g (¹/₂ cup) slivered almonds,
   toasted
30 g (1 cup) chopped parsley
6 spring onions (scallions), finely
   sliced
grated zest and juice of 1 lemon
olive oil, to drizzle
lemon wedges, to serve

Put the wild rice and stock in a saucepan, add the butter, bring to the boil, then cook, covered, over low heat for 1 hour. Drain.

Put the basmati rice in a separate saucepan with cold water and bring to the boil. Cook at a simmer for 12 minutes, then drain. Mix with the cooked wild rice and cool.

Combine the rice with the bacon, currants, almonds, parsley, spring onion and lemon zest and juice. Season, drizzle with olive oil and serve with lemon wedges.

Serves 4

Tomato caponata with mozzarella

2 small eggplants (aubergines), cubed
olive oil, for frying
1 onion, cubed
2 celery stalks, sliced
1 red capsicum (pepper), cubed
4 ripe Roma (plum) tomatoes,
   chopped
250 g (9 oz) red and 250 g (9 oz)
   yellow cherry tomatoes, halved
2 tablespoons red wine vinegar
¼ teaspoon sugar
2 tablespoons capers, rinsed
90 g (3¼ oz) unpitted black olives
400 g (14 oz) fresh mozzarella
   cheese, chopped
a large handful parsley, roughly
   chopped

Cook the eggplant in boiling salted water for 1 minute, then drain it. Squeeze out any excess moisture with your hands.

Heat 2 tablespoons of olive oil in a large frying pan and add the eggplant. Brown on all sides over a high heat, add more oil if needed. When the eggplant is cooked, take it out and drain on paper towels.

Add a little more oil to the pan, turn down the heat and cook the onion and celery for about 5 minutes, or until soft but not brown. Add the red capsicum and cook it for 2 minutes. Add the chopped tomato and a couple of tablespoons of water. Simmer the mixture for 5 minutes, or until the mixture is quite dry, then stir in the cherry tomatoes.

Season the mixture well with black pepper. Add the red wine vinegar, sugar, capers and olives and cook for 4–5 minutes over a low heat. Add the drained eggplant and cook for 5–10 minutes. Take the mixture off the heat and leave it to cool. Toss the mozzarella and parsley through the caponata and serve with a green salad and some bread to mop up the juices.

Serves 4

Creamy egg salad

10 large eggs, plus 1 egg yolk
3 teaspoons lemon juice
2 teaspoons Dijon mustard
70 ml olive oil
70 ml safflower oil
2 tablespoons chopped dill
30 ml (1 fl oz) crème fraîche or
   sour cream
2 tablespoons capers, rinsed and
   drained
20 g (1/3 cup) mustard or salad cress

Put the whole eggs in a saucepan of water. Bring to the boil and simmer for 10 minutes. Drain, then cool under cold water and peel.

To make the dressing, place the egg yolk, lemon juice and Dijon mustard in a food processor and season. With the motor running, slowly add the oils, drop by drop, increasing to a thin, steady stream as the mixture thickens. When combined, put the mayonnaise in a large bowl, add the dill, crème fraîche or sour cream and capers.

Chop the eggs and add to the mayonnaise. Put in a serving bowl, sprinkle over just the green tips of the mustard cress and serve.

Serves 4

Tomato and pesto bruschetta

8 thick slices ciabatta
80 ml (1/3 cup) olive oil
125 ml (1/2 cup) pesto
8 ripe Roma (plum) tomatoes
75 g (1/3 cup) mascarpone cheese

Turn the grill (broiler) to its highest setting. To make the bruschetta, brush both sides of each piece of bread with olive oil and put the bread on a baking tray. Grill for 3 minutes on each side, or until crisp and golden brown.

Spread a teaspoon of pesto over each piece of bruschetta and take them off the tray. Slice the tomatoes into four pieces lengthways and drain them for a minute on a piece of paper towel — this will stop the juice from the tomatoes making the bruschetta soggy. Put the tomato slices on the baking tray.

Grill the tomato for about 5 minutes, by which time it will start to cook and brown at the edges. When the tomato is cooked, layer four slices onto each piece of bruschetta. Put the bruschetta back on the tray and grill it for another minute to heat it through. Add a dollop of mascarpone and a little more pesto to each bruschetta and serve hot.

Serves 4

Chargrilled asparagus with salsa

3 eggs
2 tablespoons milk
1 tablespoon olive oil
2 cobs corn
1 small red onion, diced
1 red capsicum (pepper), finely
  chopped
2 tablespoons chopped fresh thyme
2 tablespoons olive oil, extra
2 tablespoons balsamic vinegar
24 fresh asparagus spears
1 tablespoon macadamia oil
toasted wholegrain bread, to serve

Beat the eggs and milk to combine. Heat the oil in a non-stick frying pan, add the egg and cook over a medium heat until just set. Flip and cook the other side. Remove and allow to cool, then roll up and cut into thick slices.

Cook the corn on a chargrill (griddle) or in boiling water until tender. Set aside to cool slightly, then slice off the corn kernels. Make the salsa by gently combining the corn, onion, capsicum, thyme, olive oil and balsamic vinegar.

Trim off any woody ends from the asparagus, lightly brush with macadamia oil and cook on the chargrill until tender. Serve the asparagus topped with a little salsa and the finely shredded egg, accompanied by fingers of buttered, toasted wholegrain bread.

Serves 4–6

Fried egg and red onion wrap

1 1/2 tablespoons olive oil
3 red onions, thickly sliced
1 large red capsicum (pepper), sliced
3 tablespoons balsamic vinegar
4 eggs
4 lavash breads
4 tablespoons sour cream
sweet chilli sauce

Heat the olive oil in a non-stick frying pan and add the onion. Cook it slowly, stirring occasionally until it softens and turns translucent. Add the red capsicum and continue cooking until both the onion and capsicum are soft. Turn the heat up and stir for a minute or two, or until they start to brown, then stir in the balsamic vinegar. Remove the mixture from the pan and keep warm.

Carefully break the eggs into the frying pan, keeping them separate if you can. Cook over a gentle heat until the eggs are just set.

Heat the lavash breads in a microwave or under a grill (broiler) for a few seconds (you want them to be soft and warm). Lay the breads out on a board, spread a tablespoon of sour cream onto the centre of each, then drizzle with a little chilli sauce. Put a heap of the onion and capsicum mixture on each and top with an egg. Season with salt and pepper.

Fold in one short end of each piece of lavash bread and then roll each one up lengthways.

Serves 4

Mediterranean blt

4 small vine-ripened tomatoes, halved
1 head garlic, halved
1 tablespoon extra virgin olive oil
15 g (¼ cup) basil leaves
1 loaf Italian woodfired bread
8 slices provolone cheese
8 slices mortadella
1 bunch rocket (arugula)
extra virgin olive oil, extra
balsamic vinegar

Preheat the oven to 200°C (400°F/
Gas 6). Place the tomato and garlic
in a roasting pan and drizzle with
the oil. Sprinkle with sea salt and
cracked black pepper and roast for
40 minutes, or until the garlic is soft
and the tomatoes are slightly dried.
Add the basil leaves and continue
cooking for 5 minutes, or until the
leaves are crisp. Remove from
the oven.

Cut four thick slices from the loaf
of woodfired bread and lightly toast
on both sides. Peel the roasted
garlic cloves and spread half onto
the toast. Top with the provolone,
mortadella, rocket, basil and roasted
tomatoes. Sprinkle with the remaining
roasted garlic, drizzle with extra olive
oil and the balsamic vinegar and
serve immediately.

Serves 4

Mini sweet potato and leek frittatas

1 kg (2 lb 4 oz) orange sweet potato
1 tablespoon olive oil
30 g (1 oz) butter
4 leeks, white part only, thinly sliced
2 garlic cloves, crushed
250 g (1²/₃ cup) feta cheese,
    crumbled
8 eggs
125 ml (¹/₂ cup) cream

Preheat the oven to 180°C (350°F/ Gas 4). Grease twelve 125 ml (¹/₂ cup) muffin tin holes. Cut small rounds of baking paper and place into the base of each hole. Cut the sweet potato into small cubes and boil, steam or microwave until tender. Drain well and set aside.

Heat the oil and butter in a large frying pan, add the leek and cook for about 10 minutes, stirring occasionally, or until very soft and lightly golden. Add the garlic and cook for 1 minute more. Cool, then stir in the feta and sweet potato. Divide the mixture evenly among the muffin holes.

Whisk the eggs and cream together and season with salt and freshly ground black pepper. Pour the egg mixture into each hole until three-quarters filled, then press the vegetables down gently. Bake for 25–30 minutes, or until golden and set. Leave in the tins for 5 minutes, then ease out with a knife and cool on a wire rack before serving.

Makes 12

Thai chicken with glass noodles

4 tablespoons coconut cream
1 tablespoon fish sauce
1 tablespoon palm sugar
2 chicken breasts, skinned and
  cut into shreds
120 g (4½ oz) glass noodles
2 stems lemon grass
4 makrut (kaffir lime) leaves
1 red onion, finely chopped
a large handful coriander (cilantro)
  leaves, chopped
a large handful mint, chopped
1–2 red chillies, sliced
3 green bird's eye chillies, finely sliced
2 tablespoons roasted peanuts,
  chopped
1–2 limes, cut in halves or quarters

Mix the coconut cream in a small saucepan or a wok with the fish sauce and palm sugar and bring to the boil, then add the chicken and simmer until the chicken is cooked through. This should only take a minute if you stir it a couple of times. Leave the chicken to cool in the sauce. Soak the noodles in boiling water for a minute or two — they should turn translucent and soft when they are ready. Drain them, then, using a pair of scissors, cut them into shorter lengths.

Peel the lemon grass until you reach the first purplish ring, then trim off the root. Make two or three cuts down through the bulb-like root, finely slice across it until it starts to get harder, then throw the hard top piece away. Pull the stems out of the lime leaves by folding the leaves in half, with the shiny side inwards, and pulling down on the stalk. Roll up the leaves tightly, then slice them very finely across.

Put all the ingredients, except the lime, in a bowl with the noodles and chicken, with its sauce, and toss everything together. Now squeeze the lime pieces over the dish and toss again.

Serves 4

Steak baguette with rocket and mustardy mayo

3 tablespoons olive oil, plus extra
  for frying
1 red onion, sliced
1 teaspoon brown sugar
2 teaspoons balsamic vinegar
1 teaspoon thyme
1 tablespoon Dijon mustard
3 tablespoons mayonnaise
100 g (3½ oz) rocket (arugula)
500 g (1 lb 2 oz) beef fillet, cut into
  4 thin slices
2 thick baguettes, cut in half, or
  8 thick slices of good-quality bread
2 tomatoes, sliced

Heat 2 tablespoons oil in a small saucepan. Add the onion and cook very slowly, with the lid on, stirring occasionally, until the onion is soft but not brown. This could take up to 15 minutes. Remove the lid, add the sugar and vinegar and cook for a further 10 minutes, or until the onion is soft and just browned. Take the pan off the stove and stir in the thyme.

Meanwhile, make the mustardy mayo by mixing together well the mustard and mayonnaise in a small bowl.

Drizzle the rocket leaves with the remaining olive oil and season with salt and freshly ground black pepper.

Heat 1 tablespoon of the extra oil in a frying pan over high heat and cook the steaks for 2 minutes on each side, adding more oil if necessary. Season to taste.

To serve, put out the bread, along with separate bowls containing the onion, mustardy mayo, rocket leaves, steak and sliced tomatoes. Let everyone make their own baguette so they can get the perfect mix of all the flavours.

Serves 4

Chargrilled baby octopus

2 kg (4 lb 8 oz) baby octopus
375 ml (1½ cups) red wine
3 tablespoons balsamic vinegar
2 tablespoons soy sauce
125 ml (½ cup) sweet chilli sauce
50 g (1 cup) Thai basil leaves,
   to serve

Clean the octopus, taking care not to break the ink sacs. Place the octopus, red wine and balsamic vinegar in a large, non-aluminium saucepan and bring to the boil. Reduce the heat and simmer for 15 minutes, or until just tender. Drain and transfer to a bowl. Add the soy sauce and sweet chilli sauce.

Heat a barbecue chargrill (griddle) to high and cook the octopus until it is sticky and slightly charred. Serve on a bed of Thai basil leaves.

Serves 4

Beef salad with sweet and sour cucumber

2 Lebanese (short) cucumbers
4 teaspoons caster (superfine) sugar
80 ml (1/3 cup) red wine vinegar
1 tablespoon oil
2 large or 4 small fillet steaks, cut into strips
8 spring onions (scallions), cut into pieces
2 garlic cloves, crushed
2 tablespoons ginger, grated
2 tablespoons soy sauce
4 handfuls mixed lettuce leaves

Halve the cucumber lengthways, then thinly slice and put in a colander. Sprinkle with a little bit of salt and leave for about 10 minutes. This will draw out any excess moisture and stop the final flavour from tasting watery.

Meanwhile, put 2 teaspoons each of the sugar and the vinegar in a bowl and stir until the sugar dissolves. Rinse the salt then drain the cucumber very thoroughly before dabbing it with a piece of paper towel to soak up any leftover moisture. Mix the cucumber with the vinegar mixture.

Heat half the oil in a frying pan until it is smoking. Add half the steak and fry for a minute. Remove from the pan and repeat with the remaining oil and steak. Return to the same pan, then add the spring onion and fry for another minute. Add the garlic and ginger, toss everything around once, then add the soy sauce and remaining sugar and vinegar. Cook until the sauce turns sticky then quickly remove from the heat.

Put a handful of lettuce leaves on four plates and divide the beef among them. Scatter some cucumber on the beef and serve the rest on the side.

Serves 4

Individual herbed lemon ricotta

500 g (1 lb 2 oz) ricotta cheese

Dressing
2 tablespoons olive oil
1 garlic clove, crushed
zest of 1 lemon
2 tablespoons lemon juice
1 tablespoon balsamic vinegar
125 ml (½ cup) olive oil
150 g (5½ oz) semi-dried
  (sun-blushed) tomatoes,
  roughly chopped
4 tablespoons parsley, chopped

crusty bread, to serve

Lightly grease and line four 125 ml (½ cup) ramekins with plastic wrap. Divide the ricotta between the moulds and press down firmly. Cover with plastic wrap and refrigerate for 2 hours.

Preheat the oven to 220°C (425°F/ Gas 7). Unmould each ricotta onto a tray lined with baking paper and bake for 20 minutes, or until golden.

To make the dressing, combine all the ingredients in a bowl. Place the ricottas on a serving platter. Spoon a little of the dressing around each one, drizzling a little over the top.

Serves 4

Caesar salad

1½ cos (romaine) lettuces
16 thin slices baguette
310 ml (1¼ cups) olive oil
6 bacon rashers, rinds cut off,
  chopped
1 egg yolk
1 garlic clove
4 anchovy fillets
1 tablespoon lemon juice
Worcestershire sauce, to taste
a lump of Parmesan cheese

Tear the cos lettuce into pieces and put them in a large bowl. Turn on the grill (broiler).

Brush the slices of baguette on both sides with some of the oil and grill them until they are golden brown all over. Leave to cool.

Fry the bacon in a little oil until it browns and then sprinkle it over the bowl of lettuce.

Put the egg yolk, garlic and anchovies in a blender and whizz for a minute, then with the motor still running, add the remaining oil in a steady stream through the top hole. The oil and egg should thicken immediately and form mayonnaise. Add the lemon juice and Worcestershire sauce, stir well and season with salt and pepper.

Using a potato peeler, make some Parmesan curls by running the peeler along one edge of the cheese. Try to make the curls as thin as possible.

Pour the dressing over the lettuce, add the Parmesan curls and toss everything together well. Divide the salad among four bowls and arrange the slices of toasted baguette on each one.

Serves 4

Barbecued sweet chilli seafood on banana mats

500 g (1 lb 2 oz) green prawns (shrimp), peeled and deveined, tails left intact
300 g (10½ oz) scallop meat
500 g (1 lb 2 oz) baby squid, cleaned and hoods cut in quarters
500 g (1 lb 2 oz) baby octopus, cleaned
250 ml (1 cup) sweet chilli sauce
1 tablespoon fish sauce
2 tablespoons lime juice
3 tablespoons peanut oil
banana leaves, cut into squares, to serve
lime wedges, to serve

Place the prawns, scallops, squid and the octopus in a shallow, non-metallic bowl.

In a separate bowl combine the sweet chilli sauce, fish sauce, lime juice and 1 tablespoon of the peanut oil. Pour the mixture over the seafood and mix gently to coat. Allow to marinate for 1 hour. Drain the seafood well and reserve the marinade.

Heat the remaining oil on a barbecue hotplate. Cook the seafood in batches (depending on the size of your barbecue) over a high heat for 3–5 minutes, or until tender. Drizzle each batch with a little of the leftover marinade during cooking.

Pile the seafood high onto the squares of banana leaf and serve with wedges of lime, if desired.

Serves 4

Spinach and zucchini frittata

1 tablespoon olive oil
1 red onion, thinly sliced
2 zucchini (courgettes), sliced
1 garlic clove, crushed
300 g (10½ oz) baby English spinach
   leaves, stalks removed
6 eggs
2 tablespoons cream
80 g (3 oz) Emmenthal cheese, grated

Heat the oil in a medium non-stick frying pan and fry the onion and zucchini over medium heat until they are a pale golden brown. Add the garlic and cook it for a minute. Add the spinach and cook until the spinach has wilted and any excess moisture has evaporated off — if you don't do this, your frittata will end up soggy in the middle, as the liquid will continue to come out as it cooks. Shake the pan so you get an even layer of mixture. Turn the heat down to low.

Beat the eggs and cream together and season with salt and pepper. Stir in half of the cheese and pour the mixture over the spinach. Cook the bottom of the frittata for about 4 minutes, or until the egg is just set. While you are doing this, turn on the grill (broiler). When the bottom of the frittata is set, scatter on the rest of the cheese and put the frying pan under the grill to cook the top.

Turn the frittata out of the frying pan after leaving it to set for a minute. Cut it into wedges to serve.

Serves 4

Mushrooms with marinated feta

2 large oxheart tomatoes
20 fresh asparagus spears
300 g (10½ oz) marinated feta cheese
60 ml (¼ cup) extra virgin olive oil
zest of 1 lemon
2 garlic cloves, crushed
2 tablespoons lemon juice
4 large field mushrooms, brushed
  clean and stems removed
4 eggs
fresh oregano, to garnish

Cut the tomatoes into thick slices. Trim the ends from the asparagus.

Drain the oil from the feta and place into a non-metallic bowl. Stir in the olive oil, lemon zest, garlic and lemon juice. Season with cracked black pepper.

Place the mushrooms and tomatoes in a shallow dish and pour the oil mixture over them. Toss gently to coat, and marinate for 15 minutes. Drain the mushrooms, reserving the marinade, and cook them, together with the tomatoes, on a lightly oiled barbecue grill plate until tender.

Add the asparagus towards the end of cooking, and lastly the eggs. Place the mushrooms on a plate, top each one with some asparagus spears, a slice of tomato, an egg and some sliced feta. Drizzle with the oil marinade and garnish with oregano.

Serves 4

Toasted cheese, aïoli and ham sandwich

1 loaf ciabatta or Turkish bread
1 garlic clove, crushed
125 ml (1/2 cup) mayonnaise
4 slices ham
100 g (31/2 oz) semi-dried
  (sun-blushed) tomatoes, chopped
2 tablespoons capers, chopped
6–8 slices Cheddar cheese

Turn on the grill (broiler). Cut the bread in half horizontally and then into four equal pieces. Toast all the pieces. To make the aïoli, mix the garlic into the mayonnaise and season it well with salt and pepper.

Spread the aïoli over the insides of each sandwich. Put a slice of ham on four of the pieces and then divide the semi-dried tomatoes and capers among them. Top with enough cheese slices to make a good layer and put them on a baking tray.

Grill the sandwiches until the cheese melts and starts to bubble and then put the tops back on and press them down firmly.

Cut each sandwich in half diagonally and enjoy.

Serves 4

Steak sandwich with salsa verde

2 garlic cloves, crushed
4 handfuls parsley
½ bunch basil leaves
½ bunch mint leaves
3 tablespoons olive oil
2 teaspoons capers, chopped
2 teaspoons lemon juice
2 teaspoons red wine vinegar
4 minute steaks
4 large pieces ciabatta or Turkish
  bread, halved horizontally
1 Lebanese (short) cucumber, sliced

To make the salsa verde, put the garlic and herbs in a food processor with 2 tablespoons of the oil and whizz them together until they are coarsely chopped. Tip the chopped herbs into a bowl and stir in the capers, lemon juice and vinegar. Season with salt and pepper.

Heat the remaining oil in a frying pan and fry the steaks for 1 minute on each side — they should cook very quickly and start to brown.

While the steaks are cooking, toast the bread. Spread some salsa verde on all the pieces of the bread and make four sandwiches with the steaks and cucumber.

Serves 4

Pizzette

125 g (1 cup) plain (all-purpose) flour
150 g (1 cup) wholemeal plain
  (all-purpose) flour
2 teaspoons dry yeast
1/2 teaspoon sugar
1/2 teaspoon salt
2 tablespoons plain yoghurt
2 tablespoons tomato paste (purée)
1 garlic clove, crushed
1 teaspoon dried oregano
20 g (1/2 oz) lean shaved ham
2 teaspoons grated light mozzarella
  cheese
chopped rocket (arugula), to serve
extra virgin olive oil, to serve

Sift the plain flour into a bowl, then add the wholemeal plain flour, dry yeast, sugar and salt. Make a well in the centre, add 125 ml (1/2 cup) water and the yoghurt and mix to a dough. Knead on a lightly floured surface for 5 minutes, or until smooth and elastic. Cover with a tea towel and rest in a warm place for 20–30 minutes, or until doubled in size.

Preheat the oven to moderately hot 200ºC (400°F/Gas 6). Punch the dough down and knead for 30 seconds, then divide into four portions. Roll each portion into a 15 cm (6 in) round and place on a baking tray.

Combine the tomato paste, garlic, oregano and 1 tablespoon water. Spread the paste over each base then top with the ham and mozzarella. Bake for 12–15 minutes, or until crisp and golden on the edges. Just before serving, top with chopped rocket and drizzle with extra virgin olive oil.

Makes 4

Salade niçoise

8 small salad potatoes (about 600 g/
    1 lb 5 oz)
180 g (6 oz) small green beans,
    topped, tailed and halved
1 tablespoon olive oil
400 g (14 oz) tuna steak, cubed
1 garlic clove, crushed
1 teaspoon Dijon mustard
2 tablespoons white wine vinegar
125 ml (½ cup) olive oil, extra
4 handfuls green lettuce leaves
12 cherry tomatoes, halved
90 g (3¼ oz) black olives
2 tablespoons capers, drained
4 hard-boiled eggs, cut into wedges
8 anchovies, halved
lemon wedges

Cook the potatoes in boiling salted water for about 10 minutes, or until they are just tender. Drain, cut into wedges, then put them in a bowl. Cook the beans in boiling salted water for 3 minutes, then drain and hold under cold running water for a minute (this will stop them cooking any further). Add them to the potatoes.

Heat the olive oil in a frying pan and, when it is hot, cook the tuna cubes for about 3 minutes, or until they are browned on all sides. Add these cubes to the potatoes and beans.

Whisk together the garlic, mustard and vinegar, then add the extra oil in a thin, steady stream, whisking until smooth. Season well.

Cover the base of a large bowl with the lettuce leaves. Scatter the potatoes, beans, tuna, tomatoes, olives and capers over the leaves and drizzle with the dressing. Decorate with the egg wedges and anchovies. Squeeze some lemon juice over the salad.

Serves 4

Bacon and avocado salad

8 bacon rashers, rinds cut off
400 g (14 oz) green beans, topped,
  tailed and halved
300 g (10½ oz) baby English spinach
  leaves
2 French shallots, finely sliced
2 avocados
¼ teaspoon brown sugar
1 garlic clove, crushed
80 ml (⅓ cup) olive oil
1 tablespoon balsamic vinegar
1 teaspoon sesame oil

Turn on the grill (broiler). Put the bacon on a tray and grill on both sides until it is nice and crisp. Leave it to cool and then break into pieces.

Bring a saucepan of water to the boil and cook the beans for 4 minutes. Drain and then hold them under cold running water for a few seconds to stop them cooking any further.

Put the spinach in a large bowl and add the beans, bacon and shallots. Halve the avocados, then cut into cubes and add them to the bowl of salad.

Mix the brown sugar and garlic in a small bowl. Add the rest of the ingredients and whisk everything together to make a dressing.

Pour the dressing over the salad and toss well. Grind some black pepper over the top and sprinkle with some salt.

Serves 4

Goat's cheese, leek and tapenade parcels

110 g (4 oz) butter
4 leeks, thinly sliced
8 sheets filo pastry
2 tablespoons tapenade
4 small thyme sprigs
4 small rounds of goat's cheese or
    4 thick slices off a log

Turn the oven on to 180°C (350°F/ Gas 4). Melt half of the butter in a saucepan, add the leeks and stir until they are coated in the butter. Cook them slowly over a low heat until they are completely tender.

Melt the rest of the butter in a small saucepan on the stove. Place one of the sheets of filo on the work surface with the short end facing you. Brush the pastry with butter. Lay another sheet right on top of it and cover it with a tea towel to stop the pastry drying out. Do the same with the other six sheets.

When the leeks are cooked, uncover the filo. Spread a quarter of the tapenade over the middle of each piece of pastry, leaving a wide border around the edges. Divide the leeks among the filo, putting them on the tapenade. Top each pile of leek with the goat's cheese and then a thyme sprig. Now fold the bottom bit of pastry up and the two sides in, to enclose the filling, then fold the top end of the pastry down and roll the whole parcel over. Repeat with the remaining parcels. Brush the pastry with the butter and bake the parcels for 20 minutes. The pastry should be browned and the filling melted.

Serves 4

Spinach salad with chicken and sesame dressing

450 g (1 lb) baby English spinach
  leaves
1 Lebanese (short) cucumber, peeled
  and diced
4 spring onions (scallions), shredded
2 carrots, cut into matchsticks
2 chicken breasts, cooked
2 tablespoons tahini
2 tablespoons lime juice
3 teaspoons sesame oil
1 teaspoon sugar
pinch of chilli flakes
2 tablespoons sesame seeds
a large handful coriander (cilantro)
  leaves

Put the spinach in a large bowl. Scatter the cucumber, spring onion and carrot over the top. Shred the chicken breast into long pieces and scatter it over the vegetables.

Mix together the tahini, lime juice, sesame oil, sugar and chilli flakes, then add salt to taste. Drizzle this dressing over the salad.

Cook the sesame seeds in a dry frying pan over low heat for a minute or two, stirring them around. When they start to brown and smell toasted, tip them over the salad. Scatter the coriander leaves over the top. Toss the salad just before serving.

Serves 4

Chicken sandwich

2 skinless chicken breast fillets,
  cut in half horizontally
2 tablespoons olive oil
2 tablespoons lemon juice
4 large pieces ciabatta or Turkish
  bread, cut in half horizontally
1 garlic clove, cut in half
mayonnaise
1 avocado, sliced
2 tomatoes, sliced
a large handful of rocket (arugula)
  leaves, long stems snapped off

Flatten out each piece of chicken by hitting it either with your fist, the flat side of a knife blade or cleaver, or with a meat mallet. Don't break the flesh, just thin it out a bit. Trim off any fat or sinew.

Heat the oil in a frying pan, add the chicken pieces and fry them on both sides for a couple of minutes, or until they turn brown and are cooked through (you can check by cutting into the middle of one). Sprinkle with the lemon juice, then take the chicken out of the pan. Add the bread to the pan with the cut-side down and cook for a minute, pressing down on it to flatten it and help soak up any juices. Take the bread out of the pan, rub the cut side of the garlic over the surface, then spread all the pieces with a generous amount of mayonnaise. Put a piece of chicken on four of the pieces, season and then layer with the avocado and tomato, seasoning as you go. Finish with the rocket and the tops of the bread, then serve.

Serves 4

Vietnamese chicken salad

2 chicken breasts or 4 chicken thighs, cooked
2 tablespoons lime juice
1½ tablespoons fish sauce
¼ teaspoon sugar
1–2 bird's eye chillies, finely chopped
1 garlic clove, crushed
2 French shallots, finely sliced
2 handfuls bean sprouts
a large handful shredded Chinese cabbage
4 tablespoons Vietnamese mint or mint leaves, finely chopped

Take the flesh off the chicken bones and shred it. Discard the skin and bones.

Mix together the lime juice, fish sauce, sugar, chilli, garlic and shallot.

Bring a saucepan of water to the boil and throw in the bean sprouts. After 10 seconds, drain them and rinse under cold water to stop them cooking any longer.

Mix the bean sprouts with the Chinese cabbage, Vietnamese mint and chicken. Pour the dressing over the salad and toss everything together well.

Serves 4

Barbecued honey chicken wings

12 chicken wings
4 tablespoons soy sauce
3 tablespoons sherry
3 tablespoons oil
1 garlic clove, crushed
3 tablespoons honey

Rinse the chicken wings, then give them a thorough pat with paper towels to dry them. Tuck the wing tips into the underside.

Put the chicken wings in a shallow non-metallic dish. Whisk together the soy sauce, sherry, oil and garlic, then pour all over the chicken wings, lightly tossing for good measure. Cover with plastic wrap, then leave in the fridge for 2 hours to give the chicken a chance to take up some of the marinade — it will help if you turn the wings occasionally.

The honey needs to be heated enough for it to become brushing consistency — either use the microwave or warm it gently in a small saucepan.

Lightly grease a barbecue or chargrill pan (griddle) and heat it up. Lift the chicken out of the marinade and add it to the hot pan. Cook the chicken wings until tender and cooked through, turning occasionally — this should take about 12 minutes. Now brush the wings with the warmed honey and cook for 2 minutes more.

Serves 4

Bean enchiladas

1 tablespoon light olive oil
1 onion, finely sliced
3 garlic cloves, crushed
1 bird's eye chilli, finely chopped
2 teaspoons ground cumin
125 ml (½ cup) vegetable stock
3 tomatoes, peeled, seeded and
  chopped
1 tablespoon tomato paste (purée)
2 x 430 g (15 oz) cans three-bean mix
2 tablespoons chopped coriander
  (cilantro) leaves
8 flour tortillas
1 small avocado, peeled and
  chopped
125 g (½ cup) light sour cream
10 g (½ cup) coriander (cilantro)
  sprigs
116 g (2 cups) shredded lettuce

Heat the oil in a deep frying pan over medium heat. Add the onion and cook for 3–4 minutes, or until just soft. Add the garlic and chilli and cook for a further 30 seconds. Add the cumin, vegetable stock, tomato and tomato paste and cook for 6–8 minutes, or until the mixture is quite thick and pulpy. Season with salt and freshly ground black pepper.

Preheat the oven to 170°C (325°F/ Gas 3). Drain and rinse the beans. Add the beans to the sauce and cook for 5 minutes to heat through, then add the chopped coriander.

Meanwhile, wrap the tortillas in foil and warm in the oven for 3–4 minutes.

Place a tortilla on a plate and spread with ¼ cup of the bean mixture. Top with some avocado, sour cream, coriander sprigs and lettuce. Roll the enchiladas up, tucking in the ends. Cut each one in half to serve.

Serves 4

Steamed rice noodle rolls

700 g (1 lb 9 oz) barbecued or
    roast duck
8 rice noodle rolls
2 spring onions (scallions), finely
    shredded
2 thick slices fresh ginger, finely
    shredded
a handful coriander (cilantro) leaves
oyster sauce, for drizzling
chilli sauce, to serve

Cut the duck into bite-sized pieces.
You may have to strip the flesh off the
bones first, depending on how you
bought it — leave the skin on but trim
off any fatty bits.

Gently unroll the rice noodle rolls.
If they are a bit stiff, steam or
microwave them for a minute or two.
If they are in a vacuum-wrapped
package, you can also drop the
wrapped package in boiling water
for 5 minutes.

Put a pile of duck (an eighth of the
whole amount) at one edge of the
narrower end of one noodle roll and
arrange some spring onion, ginger
and coriander over it. Drizzle with
about a teaspoon of oyster sauce and
roll the sheet up. Repeat this with the
remaining sheets. Put the sheets on
a heatproof plate.

Put the plate in a bamboo or metal
steamer and set the steamer above
a saucepan filled with simmering
water. Put the lid on and steam
for 5 minutes.

Serve the rolls cut into lengths with
some more oyster sauce drizzled
over them and some chilli sauce on
the side.

Serves 4

Prawn mango salad

Dressing
2 tablespoons sour cream
175 g (6 oz) can mango purée
3 tablespoons lime juice
1 tablespoon sweet chilli sauce

6 bacon rashers, chopped
2 kg (4 lb 8 oz) cooked king prawns
  (shrimp), peeled and deveined,
  with the tails intact
3 large mangoes, peeled and cut
  into thin wedges
2 large avocados, sliced

To make the dressing, combine all the ingredients in a small bowl and whisk until smooth.

Fry the bacon until crispy, then drain on paper towels.

Arrange the prawns, mango and avocado on a large platter, then sprinkle with the bacon bits. Drizzle with the dressing, then serve.

Serves 6

Spiced parsnip and bacon cake

8 parsnips, cut into pieces
4 tablespoons butter
8 bacon rashers, rinds cut off,
   chopped
2 red chillies, finely chopped
4 French shallots, finely chopped
1½ teaspoons garam masala
2 tablespoons wholegrain mustard
1 tablespoon honey
125 ml (½ cup) cream
green salad leaves, to serve

Bring a saucepan of water to the boil and cook the parsnips at a simmer for 15 minutes. Drain them well.

Melt 2 tablespoons of the butter in a large non-stick frying pan, add the bacon and cook until browned. Add the chilli and chopped shallots and cook for 2 minutes. Stir in the garam masala and remove from the heat.

Mash the parsnips and mix them into the bacon mixture. Put the frying pan back over the heat with the last 2 tablespoons of butter, pile the parsnip mixture into the pan and flatten it out with a spatula. Cook it for a few minutes — it should hold together in a cake. Loosen the cake, slide it out onto a plate, then invert the plate back over the frying pan and flip the cake back in so you can cook the other side.

While the cake is cooking, mix the mustard, honey and cream together in a small saucepan over low heat until the mixture bubbles.

When both sides of the cake are brown, turn the cake out onto a board. Cut the cake into wedges and serve with the honey and mustard sauce and some green salad leaves.

Serves 4

Crispy lavash tiles with butter mushrooms

3 pieces lavash or Lebanese bread
2 tablespoons olive oil
25 g (1/4 cup) finely grated Parmesan cheese
100 g (3 1/2 oz) butter
4 spring onions (scallions), sliced
750 g (1 lb 10 oz) mixed mushrooms (field, button, swiss browns, pine, enoki), sliced
1 tablespoon chervil leaves

Preheat the oven to 180°C (350°F/ Gas 4). Cut the lavash bread into 3 cm (1 1/4 in) wide strips and brush lightly with 1 tablespoon of the oil. Sprinkle with the grated Parmesan cheese and bake for 10 minutes, or until crispy.

Heat the butter and the remaining oil in a large frying pan until it is sizzling. Add the spring onion and the field mushrooms and cook over a medium heat until the mushrooms are tender. Add the button, swiss brown and pine mushrooms and cook until the liquid has evaporated. Remove from the heat and stir through the enoki mushrooms.

Arrange the toasted strips of lavash bread into an interlocking square. Pile the mushrooms in the centre, garnish with chervil and serve immediately.

Serves 4

Every night

Baked chicken and leek risotto

60 g (2¼ oz) butter
1 leek, thinly sliced
2 chicken breast fillets, cut into
  small cubes
440 g (2 cups) risotto rice
60 ml (¼ cup) white wine
1.25 litres (5 cups) chicken stock
35 g (⅓ cup) grated Parmesan
  cheese
2 tablespoons thyme leaves, plus
  extra to garnish
freshly grated Parmesan cheese,
  extra

Preheat the oven to 150°C (300°F/ Gas 2) and put a 5 litre (20 cups) ovenproof dish with a lid in the oven.

Heat the butter in a saucepan over medium heat, stir in the leek and cook for about 2 minutes, then add the chicken and stir for 3 minutes. Toss in the rice and stir for 1 minute. Add the wine and stock, and bring to the boil.

Pour into the ovenproof dish and cover. Cook in the oven for 30 minutes, stirring halfway through. Remove from the oven and stir in the cheese and thyme. Season, then sprinkle with extra thyme and cheese.

Serves 4

Spaghetti carbonara

1 tablespoon olive oil
300 g (10$^1/_2$ oz) pancetta, cut into
  small dice
160 ml ($^2/_3$ cup) thick (double/heavy)
  cream
6 egg yolks
400 g (14 oz) spaghetti
65 g ($^2/_3$ cup) grated Parmesan
  cheese

Heat the olive oil in a saucepan and cook the pancetta, stirring frequently, until it is light brown and crisp. Tip the pancetta into a sieve to strain off any excess oil.

Mix the cream and egg yolks together in a bowl, and when the pancetta has cooled, add it to the egg mixture.

Cook the spaghetti in a large saucepan of boiling salted water until *al dente*, stirring once or twice to make sure the pieces are not stuck together. Drain the spaghetti and reserve a small cup of the cooking water.

Put the spaghetti back in the saucepan and put it over a low heat. Add the egg mixture and half the Parmesan, then take the pan off the heat, otherwise the egg will scramble. Season with salt and pepper and mix together. If the sauce is too thick and the pasta is stuck together, add a little of the reserved cooking water. The spaghetti should look as if it has a fine coating of egg and cream all over it.

Serve the spaghetti in warm bowls with more Parmesan sprinkled over the top.

Serves 4

Minestrone alla milanese

225 g (8 oz) dried borlotti beans
55 g (2 oz) butter
1 onion, finely chopped
1 garlic clove, finely chopped
3 tablespoons parsley, finely chopped
2 sage leaves
100 g (3½ oz) pancetta, cubed
2 celery stalks, halved, then sliced
2 carrots, sliced
3 potatoes, peeled but left whole
1 teaspoon tomato paste (purée)
400 g (14 oz) can chopped tomatoes
8 basil leaves
3 litres (12 cups) chicken or vegetable
   stock
2 zucchini (courgettes), sliced
225 g (8 oz) shelled peas
125 g (4½ oz) runner beans, cut into
   4 cm (1½ in) lengths
¼ cabbage, shredded
220 g (1 cup) risotto rice
grated Parmesan cheese, to serve

Put the dried beans in a large bowl, cover with cold water and soak overnight. Drain and rinse under cold water.

Melt the butter in a saucepan and add the onion, garlic, parsley, sage and pancetta. Cook over low heat, stirring until the onion is soft.

Add the celery, carrot and potatoes, and cook for 5 minutes. Stir in the tomato paste, tomatoes, basil and borlotti beans. Season with pepper. Add the stock and bring slowly to the boil. Cover and leave to simmer for 2 hours, stirring once or twice.

If the potatoes have not broken up, roughly break them with a fork against the side of the pan. Taste for seasoning and add the zucchini, peas, runner beans, cabbage and rice. Simmer until the rice is cooked. Serve with the Parmesan cheese.

Serves 6

Tuna mornay

60 g (2¼ oz) butter
2 tablespoons plain (all-purpose) flour
500 ml (2 cups) milk
½ teaspoon dry mustard
90 g (¾ cup) grated Cheddar cheese
600 g (1 lb 5 oz) canned tuna in
  brine, drained
2 tablespoons finely chopped parsley
2 eggs, hard-boiled and chopped
4 tablespoons fresh breadcrumbs
paprika, for dusting

Preheat the oven to 180°C (350°F/ Gas 4). Melt the butter in a small saucepan, add the flour and stir over low heat for 1 minute. Take the pan off the heat and slowly pour in the milk, stirring with your other hand until you have a smooth sauce. Return the pan to the heat and stir constantly until the sauce boils and thickens. Reduce the heat and simmer for another 2 minutes. Remove the pan from the heat, whisk in the mustard and two-thirds of the cheese — don't stop whisking until you have a smooth, rich cheesy sauce.

Roughly flake the tuna with a fork, then tip it into the cheesy sauce, along with the parsley and egg. Season with a little salt and pepper, then spoon the mixture into four 250 ml (1 cup) ovenproof ramekins.

Make the topping by mixing together the breadcrumbs and the rest of the cheese, then sprinkle it over the mornay. Add a hint of colour by dusting the top very lightly with paprika. Place in the oven until the topping is golden brown, about 20 minutes.

Serves 4

Eggplant parmigiana

1.5 kg (3 lb 5 oz) eggplants
 (aubergines)
plain (all-purpose) flour, seasoned with
 salt and pepper
350 ml (12 fl oz) olive oil
500 ml (2 cups) tomato passata or
 tomato pasta sauce
2 tablespoons roughly torn basil
 leaves
250 g (9 oz) mozzarella cheese,
 chopped
90 g (1 cup) grated Parmesan cheese

Thinly slice the eggplant lengthways. Layer the slices in a large colander, sprinkling salt between each layer. Leave for 1 hour to degorge. Rinse and pat the slices dry on both sides with paper towels, then coat lightly with the flour.

Preheat the oven to 180°C (350°F/ Gas 4) and grease a shallow 2.5 litre (10 cups) baking dish.

Heat 125 ml ($\frac{1}{2}$ cup) of the olive oil in a large frying pan. Quickly fry the eggplant slices in batches over high heat until crisp and golden on both sides. Add more olive oil as needed and drain on paper towels as you remove each batch from the pan.

Make a slightly overlapping layer of eggplant slices over the base of the dish. Season with pepper and a little salt. Spoon 4 tablespoons of passata over the eggplant and scatter some of the basil over the top. Sprinkle with some mozzarella, followed by some Parmesan. Continue layering until you have used up all the ingredients, finishing with a layer of the cheeses.

Bake for 30 minutes. Remove from the oven and allow to cool for 30 minutes before serving.

Serves 8

Pizza margherita

2 packets pizza base mix, or
  2 ready-made bases
8 very ripe Roma (plum) tomatoes
a handful basil leaves
4 garlic cloves, crushed
2 tablespoons tomato passata or
  tomato pasta sauce
5 tablespoons olive oil
400 g (14 oz) fresh mozzarella
  cheese, chopped

If you are using a packet mix, make up the pizza base following the instructions on the packet and leave it to prove. Heat the oven to as high as it will go — pizzas should cook as quickly as possible.

Remove the cores, seeds and juices from the tomatoes, chop the tomatoes roughly, then purée them in a food processor with 8 basil leaves. Stir in the garlic, passata and 2 tablespoons of olive oil and season well.

Roll out the pizza bases to 30 cm (12 in) circles and put them on oiled baking trays — if they shrink when you move them, just stretch them out again. Drizzle each with a little of the olive oil. Spoon the tomato sauce over the base, spreading it up to the rim. Scatter the mozzarella over the top and drizzle with a little more olive oil.

Cook the pizza for 5–12 minutes (this will depend on how hot your oven is), or until the base is light brown and crisp and the topping is cooked. Before serving, drizzle with a little more oil and scatter the remaining basil over the top.

Makes 2 large

Mushroom soup

2 tablespoons butter
1 onion, finely chopped
12 large (about 1.4 kg/3 lb 3 oz) field
   mushrooms, finely chopped
2 garlic cloves, crushed
2 tablespoons dry sherry
1 litre (4 cups) chicken or vegetable
   stock
2 tablespoons parsley, finely chopped
cream

Melt the butter in a large saucepan
and fry the onion until the onion
is translucent but not browned.
Add the mushroom and garlic
and continue frying. Initially the
mushrooms might give off a lot of
liquid, so keep frying until it is all
absorbed back into the mixture.
This will take 15–20 minutes.

Add the sherry to the pan, turn up
the heat and let the mixture bubble —
this burns off the alcohol but leaves
the flavour. Cool slightly, then transfer
to a blender. Whizz together until a
smooth paste forms, then add the
stock and blend until smooth. Add the
parsley and a couple of tablespoons
of cream and blend together. Pour
back into the saucepan and heat
gently. Serve with bread.

Serves 4

Prawns with garlic and chilli

125 ml (1/2 cup) olive oil
6 garlic cloves, crushed
1 red onion, finely chopped
3–4 dried chillies, cut in half, seeds
  removed
1.125 kg (about 32) large prawns
  (shrimp), peeled and deveined,
  tails left intact
4 tomatoes, finely chopped
a handful parsley or coriander
  (cilantro), chopped

Heat the oil in a large frying pan or shallow casserole. Add the garlic, onion and chilli, cook for a few minutes, then add the prawns and cook them for about 4 minutes, by which time they should be pink all over.

When the prawns are cooked, add the tomato and cook for a minute or two. Season with salt and stir the herbs through. Take the pan to the table, remembering to put it on a heatproof mat. Eat with bread to mop up the juices.

Serves 4

Imam bayildi

2 eggplants (aubergines)
5 tablespoons olive oil
2 medium onions, chopped
2 garlic cloves, crushed
6 ripe tomatoes, chopped
1 teaspoon ground cinnamon
a large handful parsley, chopped
500 ml (2 cups) tomato juice
thick plain yoghurt

Preheat the oven to 200°C (400°F/ Gas 6). Cut the eggplant in half lengthways. To hollow out the middle, run a small sharp knife around the edge of each cut half, about 1 cm (1/2 in) from the skin. Dig out the flesh in the middle, within the cut line, to leave four shells. Keep the flesh and chop it finely.

Heat 4 tablespoons of the oil in a frying pan and fry the eggplant flesh, onion and garlic until the onion is soft and cooked through. Add the tomato and any juices and stir everything together. Season with salt and pepper and add the cinnamon. Cook the mixture until it is dryish, then stir in the parsley.

Fill the eggplant shells with the mixture and put them in a large baking dish. Pour the tomato juice around the eggplant — this will help stop the eggplant drying out as it cooks. Drizzle with the remaining oil.

Bake the eggplant shells for 1 hour and 10 minutes, by which time the flesh should be tender and the filling brown on top. Serve with some of the tomato juice spooned over and a dollop of yoghurt on top.

Serves 4

Sausages cooked with lentils

3 tablespoons olive oil
8 Italian sausages
1 onion, chopped
3 garlic cloves, thinly sliced
2 tablespoons finely chopped
  rosemary
800 g (1 lb 12 oz) can tomatoes
16 juniper berries, lightly crushed
1 teaspoon freshly grated nutmeg
1 bay leaf
1 dried chilli
200 ml (7 fl oz) red wine
100 g (3½ oz) green lentils
extra rosemary, to garnish

Heat the olive oil in a large saucepan and cook the sausages for 5–10 minutes, browning well all over. Remove the sausages and set aside.

Reduce the heat to low, add the onion and garlic to the pan and cook until the onion is soft and translucent, but not browned. Stir in the rosemary, then add the tomatoes and cook gently until the sauce has thickened.

Add the juniper berries, nutmeg, bay leaf, chilli, red wine and 400 ml (14 fl oz) water. Bring to the boil, then add the lentils and the cooked sausages. Stir well, cover the saucepan and simmer gently for about 40 minutes, or until the lentils are soft. Stir the lentils a few times to prevent them sticking to the base of the pan and add a little more water if you need to cook them for a bit longer. Remove the bay leaf and chilli before serving. Garnish with rosemary.

Serves 4

Rice noodles with beef, black beans and capsicums

300 g (10½ oz) rump steak
1 garlic clove, crushed
3 tablespoons oyster sauce
2 teaspoons sugar
2 tablespoons soy sauce
5 tablespoons black bean sauce
2 teaspoons cornflour (cornstarch)
3/4 teaspoon sesame oil
1.2 kg (2 lb 11 oz) fresh or 600 g
  (1 lb 5 oz) dried flat rice noodles
1½ tablespoons oil
2 red capsicums (peppers), sliced
1 green capsicum (pepper), sliced
a handful coriander (cilantro) leaves

Cut the steak across the grain into thin slices and put it in a bowl with the garlic, oyster sauce, sugar, soy sauce, black bean sauce, cornflour and sesame oil. Mix everything together, making sure the slices are all well coated.

If you are using dried rice noodles, soak them in boiling water for 10 minutes, or until they are opaque and soft. If your noodles are particularly dry, they may need a little longer. Drain the noodles.

Heat the oil in a wok or frying pan and, when it is hot, add the capsicums. Stir-fry the capsicums for a minute or two until they are starting to soften, then add the meat mixture and cook for a minute. Add the noodles and toss everything together well. Keep cooking until the meat is cooked through and everything is hot, then toss in the coriander leaves and stir once before turning off the heat. Serve straight away.

Serves 4

Cheesy bubble and squeak cakes with bacon

4 large or 8 small floury potatoes
2 tablespoons milk
2 tablespoons butter
480 g (1 lb) savoy cabbage, shredded
120 g (4 oz) Cheddar cheese, grated
1 tablespoon oil
8 bacon rashers, rinds cut off

Cut the potatoes into pieces and cook them in simmering water for 15 minutes, or until they are soft. Drain well, put them back in the pan with the milk and mash until they are smooth. Season with salt and pepper.

Melt the butter in a non-stick frying pan and cook the cabbage until it is soft. Add this to the potato along with the cheese. The mixture should be stiff enough to form the potato into cakes — it is up to you whether you make large ones or small ones.

Heat the oil in the same frying pan over a medium heat and cook the bacon on both sides until it is crisp. Remove the bacon from the pan, keep warm. Add the potato cakes to the pan and fry them on both sides until they are well browned and slightly crisp. Shake the pan occasionally to move the cakes around so they don't stick. Serve with the bacon.

Serves 4

Saffron fish cakes with herb crème fraîche

160 ml (²/₃ cup) milk
2 pinches saffron threads
500 g (about 4 medium fillets) white fish fillets
4 large potatoes, cut into chunks
2 garlic cloves, unpeeled
2 tablespoons plain (all-purpose) flour
2 teaspoons grated lemon zest
a handful parsley, finely chopped
2 tablespoons cream
80 ml (¹/₃ cup) crème fraîche
2 tablespoons mint, finely chopped
2 tablespoons parsley, finely chopped
1–2 tablespoons butter

Put the milk and saffron in a frying pan and heat until simmering. Add the fish, turn up the heat a little and cook until the fish turns opaque and flaky — you might need to turn it over halfway through. Don't worry if it breaks up. Lift the fish out of the milk into a bowl and break it up roughly with a fork. Keep the milk.

Cook the potato and garlic clove in simmering water for about 12 minutes, or until the potato is tender. Drain the potato and put it back in the saucepan. Peel the garlic and add it to the potato, mash everything together and strain in the saffron milk. Keep mashing until the mixture is smooth, then stir in the fish, flour, 1 teaspoon of the lemon zest, the parsley and cream. Season well.

Shape the mixture into eight even-sized cakes. Put them in the fridge to chill while you make the herb crème fraîche by mixing together the crème fraîche, remaining lemon zest and herbs.

Heat the butter in a large non-stick frying pan and cook the fish cakes for 3 minutes on each side — they should have a brown crust. Serve with the crème fraîche.

Serves 4

Stir-fried chicken with ginger and cashews

1½ tablespoons oil

8 spring onions (scallions), cut into pieces

3 garlic cloves, crushed

8 cm (3 in) piece ginger, finely shredded

2 skinless chicken breasts, cut into strips

2 red capsicums (peppers), cut into strips

150 g (5½ oz) snow peas (mangetout)

100 g (3½ oz) cashews

2 tablespoons soy sauce

1½ teaspoons sesame oil

Heat the oil in a wok until it is smoking — this will only take a few seconds. Add the spring onion, garlic and ginger and stir them around for a few seconds. Next, add the chicken and stir it around until it has all turned white. Add the red capsicum and keep stirring, then throw in the snow peas and cashews and stir-fry for another minute or so.

Once the red capsicum has started to soften a little, add the soy sauce and sesame oil, toss everything together and then tip the stir-fry out into a serving dish.

Serve with rice or noodles and more soy sauce if you like.

Serves 4

Minestrone with pesto

1 tablespoon olive oil
1 small onion, finely chopped
1 garlic clove, finely chopped
1 tablespoon finely chopped parsley
55 g (2 oz) pancetta, cubed
1 celery stalk, halved, then sliced
1 carrot, sliced
1 teaspoon tomato paste (purée)
200 g (7 oz) canned chopped
    tomatoes
1 litre (4 cups) chicken or vegetable
    stock
1 zucchini (courgette), sliced
2 tablespoons peas
6 runner beans, cut into 2 cm
    ($^3/_4$ in) lengths
a handful shredded savoy cabbage
2 tablespoons ditalini
100 g (3$^1/_2$ oz) canned borlotti beans,
    drained and rinsed
2 tablespoons fresh pesto

Melt the oil in a large saucepan and add the onion, garlic, parsley and pancetta. Cook everything over a very low heat, stirring the mixture once or twice, for about 10 minutes, or until the onion is soft and golden. If your heat won't go very low, keep an eye on everything and stir more often.

Add the celery and carrot and cook them for 5 minutes. Stir in the tomato paste and chopped tomato with plenty of pepper. Add the stock and bring slowly to the boil. Cover and leave to simmer for 30 minutes, stirring once or twice.

Taste the soup for seasoning, adjust if necessary, then add the zucchini, peas, runner beans, cabbage, ditalini and borlotti beans. Simmer everything for a couple of minutes until the pasta is *al dente*. Serve with some pesto spooned into the middle of each bowl of minestrone.

Serves 4

Spaghetti puttanesca

400 g (14 oz) spaghetti
2 tablespoons olive oil
1 onion, finely chopped
2 garlic cloves, finely sliced
1 small red chilli, cored, seeded and
  sliced
6 anchovy fillets, finely chopped
400 g (14 oz) canned chopped
  tomatoes
1 tablespoon fresh oregano, finely
  chopped
16 black olives, halved and pitted
2 tablespoons baby capers
a handful basil leaves

Cook the spaghetti in a large saucepan of boiling salted water until *al dente*, stirring once or twice to make sure the pieces are not stuck together. The cooking time will vary depending on the brand of spaghetti. Check the pasta occasionally as it cooks because the time given on packet instructions is often too long by a minute or two.

Heat the olive oil in a large saucepan and add the onion, garlic and chilli. Gently fry for about 8 minutes, or until the onion is soft. Add the anchovies and cook for another minute. Add the tomato, oregano, olive halves and capers and bring to the boil. Reduce the heat, season with salt and pepper, and leave the sauce to simmer for 3 minutes.

Drain the spaghetti and add it to the sauce. Toss together well so that the pasta is coated in the sauce. Scatter the basil over the top and serve.

Serves 4

Prawn laksa

1½ tablespoons oil
4 tablespoons laksa paste
500 ml (2 cups) coconut milk
500 ml (2 cups) chicken stock
16 prawns (shrimp), peeled and
  deveined
250 g (4 bundles) rice vermicelli
8 bean curd puffs, cut into 3 pieces
10 cm (4 in) piece cucumber, cut
  into shreds
4 handfuls bean sprouts
a few sprigs Vietnamese mint or
  mint leaves
sambal oelek
lime wedges

Heat the oil in a wok or saucepan and add the laksa paste (depending on the brand, you may need to add a little more or less than the recipe says — you can only find this out by trial and error, so start with a little, make up the soup base and then stir in a bit more if you need to). Cook the paste over a medium heat, stirring it to stop it from sticking, for 2 to 3 minutes.

Stir in the coconut milk and chicken stock, bring the mixture to the boil and simmer for 5 minutes. Add the prawns, bring the mixture back to the boil, then reduce the heat and simmer for 3 minutes — the prawns will turn pink and opaque when they are ready.

Cook the rice vermicelli in boiling water for 3 minutes. Drain and divide among four deep serving bowls.

Divide the bean curd puffs, cucumber and bean sprouts among the bowls, then ladle in the laksa mixture. Garnish the laksa with a sprig or two of Vietnamese mint and a small amount of sambal oelek (be careful as it is very hot). Serve with lime wedges to squeeze into the laksa.

Serves 4

Asparagus risotto

1 kg (2 lb 4 oz) asparagus
1 litre (4 cups) chicken stock
4 tablespoons olive oil
1 onion, finely chopped
360 g (1²/₃ cups) risotto rice
85 g (3 oz) Parmesan cheese, grated
3 tablespoons thick (double/heavy)
   cream

Wash the asparagus and remove the woody ends. Separate the tender tips from the stems.

Cook the asparagus stems in boiling water for about 8 minutes, or until very tender. Drain and put in a blender with the chicken stock. Blend for 1 minute, then put in a saucepan, bring to the boil and maintain at a low simmer.

Cook the asparagus tips in boiling water for 1 minute, drain and refresh in iced water.

Heat the olive oil in a wide, heavy-based saucepan. Add the onion and cook until softened but not browned. Add the rice and reduce the heat to low. Season and stir briefly to thoroughly coat the rice. Stir in a ladleful of the simmering stock and cook over moderate heat, stirring continuously. When the stock has been absorbed, stir in another ladleful. Continue this process for about 20 minutes, until all the stock has been added and the rice is *al dente*.

Add the Parmesan cheese and cream, and gently stir in the asparagus tips. Season with salt and pepper, and serve hot.

Serves 4

Baked potatoes with rocket, broad beans and blue cheese

4 large potatoes
coarse salt
300 g (10½ oz) broad (fava) beans
80 ml (⅓ cup) cream
120 g (4 oz) blue cheese, crumbled
4 handfuls rocket (arugula), chopped

Put the oven on to 200°C (400°F/ Gas 6). Wash the potatoes and, while they are still damp, rub them with a little of the coarse salt. Prick them several times and then put them in the oven, sitting directly on the oven shelf. This will help them get a good all-round heat. Bake for 1 hour, then squeeze them gently — they should be soft. If they are still hard, give them another 15 minutes or so.

Cook the broad beans in boiling water for 3 minutes, then drain them well. Peel off the outer grey skins.

When the potatoes are cooked, cut a cross in one side of each and squeeze the potatoes around the middle until they open up.

Put the cream in a small saucepan, add the broad beans, cook them gently for a minute or two, then add the blue cheese and rocket. Stir everything together and when the rocket has wilted, spoon the mixture into the potatoes. Season with black pepper.

Serves 4

Salmon kedgeree

1 litre (4 cups) fish stock
400 g (14 oz) salmon fillet
3 tablespoons butter
2 tablespoons oil
1 onion, chopped
2 teaspoons madras curry paste
200 g (1 cup) long-grain rice
2 hard-boiled eggs, cut into wedges
3 tablespoons chopped parsley
  leaves
3 tablespoons cream
lemon wedges, to serve

Put the stock in a frying pan and bring to the boil. Put the salmon in the stock, cover, then reduce the heat to a simmer. Cook for 3 minutes, or until it becomes firm when pressed and turns opaque. Lift out the salmon and flake it into large pieces by gently pulling it apart with your hands.

Melt half of the butter in a frying pan with the oil, add the onion and cook over a low heat until the onion softens and turns translucent. Stir in the curry paste, then add the rice and mix well until the rice is coated. Add the fish stock, mix well, then bring the mixture to the boil.

Simmer the rice, covered, over a very low heat for 8 minutes, then add the salmon and cook, covered, for another 5 minutes, until all the liquid is absorbed. If the rice is too dry and not cooked, add a splash of boiling water and keep cooking for a further 1–2 minutes.

Stir in the rest of the butter, the eggs, parsley and cream (you can leave out the cream if you prefer — the results won't be so rich). Serve the kedgeree with the lemon wedges to squeeze over.

Serves 4

Spicy sausages with harissa and couscous

2 tablespoons butter
300 g (1 ½ cups) instant couscous
2 teaspoons harissa
60 ml (¼ cup) olive oil
2 tablespoons lemon juice
1 ½ tablespoons grated lemon zest
2 tablespoons parsley, chopped
150 g (5½ oz) chargrilled red
  capsicum (pepper), sliced
40 g (⅓ cup) raisins
12 merguez sausages
thick plain yoghurt, to serve

Put the butter in a saucepan with 500 ml (2 cups) water and bring to the boil. Sprinkle in the couscous, mix it into the water, then take it off the stove. Put a lid on the pan and leave it to sit for 5 minutes. Turn on the grill (broiler). Stir the harissa, olive oil, lemon juice and zest together until well mixed. Add the parsley, red capsicum and raisins and leave everything to marinate briefly.

Grill the sausages for 8 minutes, turning them so they brown on all sides.

Meanwhile, take the lid off the couscous, stir it for a minute or two to separate the grains, then stir in the harissa mixture.

Serve the couscous with the sausages sliced over it and topped with a large dollop of yoghurt.

Serves 4

Roast tomato risotto

1 litre (4 cups) chicken or vegetable
  stock
a pinch saffron threads
250 ml (1 cup) dry white wine
2 tablespoons butter
1 onion, finely chopped
270 g (1⅓ cups) risotto rice
1 tablespoon olive oil
1 garlic clove, crushed
400 g (about 40) cherry tomatoes
Parmesan cheese, grated
4 tablespoons parsley, finely chopped

Heat the stock in a saucepan until it is simmering, then leave it over a low heat. Put the saffron into the wine and leave it to soak.

Melt the butter in a large, deep heavy-based frying pan, then gently cook the onion until it is soft, but not browned. Add the rice, turn the heat to low and stir well to coat all the grains of rice in the butter.

Add the wine and saffron to the rice, turn the heat up to medium and cook, stirring the rice, until all the liquid has been absorbed. Add the hot stock, a couple of ladles at a time, stirring continuously so that the rice cooks evenly and releases some of its starch.

While the rice is cooking, heat the oil in a saucepan, add the garlic and tomatoes, then fry for 2 to 3 minutes over medium heat until the tomatoes are slightly soft and have burst open. Season well.

Once all the stock has been added to the rice, taste the rice to see if it is *al dente*. Stir in 4 tablespoons of Parmesan and the parsley. Spoon the tomatoes over the top and scatter more Parmesan on top. Serve straight away.

Serves 4

Hamburgers with fresh corn relish

700 g (1 lb 9 oz) minced (ground) beef
1 garlic clove
1½ onions, very finely chopped
2 tablespoons parsley, finely chopped
1 tablespoon tomato ketchup
¼ teaspoon Worcestershire sauce
2 corn cobs
2 tomatoes, finely chopped
1 tablespoon sweet chilli sauce
a handful coriander (cilantro) leaves
lime juice
1 tablespoon oil
4 buns
baby cos (romaine) leaves

Turn on the grill (broiler). Put the beef in a bowl with the garlic, half of the onion, the parsley, tomato ketchup and the Worcestershire sauce. Season and mix well, then leave it to marinate while you make the relish.

Grill the corn cob on all sides until it is slightly blackened and charred around the edges. By this time it should be cooked through. Slice off the kernels by slicing down the length of the cob with a sharp knife. Mix the kernels with the tomato, chilli sauce, coriander and remaining onion. Add lime juice and salt and pepper, to taste.

Form the beef mixture into four large patties and flatten them out to the size of the buns (bear in mind that they will shrink as they cook).

Heat the oil in a frying pan and fry the beef patties for between 3 and 5 minutes on each side, depending on how well cooked you like them. While they are cooking, toast the buns.

Lay a lettuce leaf or two on each bun bottom, add some relish and top with a hamburger patty and the bun top. Serve any extra relish on the side.

Serves 4

Roast baby potatoes with sweet chilli dip

600 g (1 lb 5 oz) baby potatoes
1$\frac{1}{2}$ tablespoons olive oil
2 teaspoons thyme leaves
2 teaspoons coarse salt
80 ml ($\frac{1}{3}$ cup) sweet chilli sauce
80 ml ($\frac{1}{3}$ cup) sour cream
2 spring onions (scallions), finely
  chopped

Put the oven on to 200°C (400°F/ Gas 6). If any of your potatoes are too big to eat in more than two bites, cut them in half. Put them in a roasting tin with the oil, thyme and salt and mix them around so they are all coated. Roast for 30 to 40 minutes, or until the potatoes are cooked through.

Mix the sweet chilli sauce, sour cream and spring onion together. Serve with the potatoes for dipping.

Serves 4

Tandoori chicken with cardamom rice

250 ml (1 cup) natural yoghurt, plus
    extra for serving
60 g (¼ cup) tandoori paste
2 tablespoons lemon juice
1 kg (2 lb 4 oz) chicken breast fillets,
    cut into 4 cm (1½ in) cubes
1 tablespoon oil
1 onion, finely diced
300 g (1½ cups) long-grain rice
2 cardamom pods, bruised
750 ml (3 cups) hot chicken stock
400 g (14 oz) English spinach leaves

Soak eight wooden skewers in water for 30 minutes to prevent them burning during cooking. Combine the yoghurt, tandoori paste and lemon juice in a non-metallic dish. Add the chicken and coat well, then cover and marinate for at least 10 minutes.

Meanwhile, heat the oil in a saucepan. Add the onion and cook for 3 minutes, then add the rice and cardamom pods. Cook, stirring often, for 3–5 minutes, or until the rice is slightly opaque. Add the hot chicken stock and bring to the boil. Reduce the heat to low, cover, and cook the rice, without removing the lid, for 15 minutes.

Heat a barbecue plate or oven grill (broiler) to very hot. Thread the chicken cubes onto the skewers, leaving the bottom quarter of the skewers empty. Cook on each side for 5 minutes, or until cooked through.

Wash the spinach and put in a large saucepan with just the water clinging to the leaves. Cook, covered, over medium heat for 1–2 minutes, or until the spinach has wilted. Uncover the rice, fluff up with a fork and serve with the spinach, chicken and extra yoghurt.

Serves 4

Grilled eggplant with ricotta and tomato

2 eggplants (aubergines), sliced
80 ml (⅓ cup) olive oil
500 g (1 lb 2 oz) cherry tomatoes, halved
2 garlic cloves, crushed
2 teaspoons capers, drained
125 g (4½ oz) ricotta cheese
a few small basil leaves

Heat the grill (broiler) to high. Brush the eggplant slices with some of the oil. Grill the slices on both sides until they are brown, then lay them in a large shallow baking dish (choose one that will fit under the grill).

Heat the rest of the oil in a small saucepan, tip in the cherry tomatoes and garlic, then fry briefly until the tomatoes just start to soften. Add the capers for a minute. Tip the tomatoes over the eggplant, season well and spoon the ricotta on top. Put the dish back under the grill until the ricotta starts to bubble, then scatter the basil over the top.

Serves 4

Ham braised with witlof

1½ tablespoons oil
2 teaspoons butter
4 witlof (chicory/Belgian endive)
   heads, sliced horizontally
8 thick slices leg ham
2 teaspoons brown sugar
180 ml (¾ cup) white wine
2 tablespoons chopped parsley

Heat the oil in a large frying pan, add the butter and when it is sizzling, add the witlof, with the cut-side down, and fry for a minute. Add the slices of ham to the pan and fry them briefly on each side, moving the witlof to one side. Add the sugar and wine to the pan, season well and cover it with a lid. Cook for about 3 minutes, or until the witlof is soft.

Take the lid off the pan, turn the heat up and let the sauce bubble until it has thickened and gone quite sticky. Stir in the parsley.

Serves 4

Cauliflower rarebit

8 thick slices ciabatta
1 garlic clove
800 g (1 lb 12 oz) cauliflower, cut into
  small florets
120 g (1 cup) grated Gruyère cheese
120 g (1 cup) grated Cheddar cheese
1 tablespoon Dijon mustard
2 eggs, beaten
2 tablespoons beer
4 tablespoons cream

Turn on the grill (broiler) and toast the ciabatta. Cut the garlic clove in half and rub the cut sides over one side of each slice of ciabatta.

Bring a saucepan of water to the boil and cook the cauliflower for about 5 minutes, or until it is tender when you prod it with a knife. Drain it very well.

Mix the cheeses, mustard, egg, beer and cream together. Put the toast on a baking tray and arrange some cauliflower on top of each piece. Divide the cheese mixture among the pieces of toast, making sure you coat all the cauliflower.

Put the rarebits under the grill and grill them until they are brown and bubbling.

Serves 4

Chicken casserole with olives and tomatoes

1 tablespoon olive oil
1 large onion, chopped
2 garlic cloves, crushed
8 pieces chicken, skin on
1 tablespoon tomato paste (purée)
375 ml (1½ cups) white wine
a pinch of sugar
8 large ripe tomatoes, chopped
4 tablespoons parsley, chopped
180 g (6½ oz) green beans, topped, tailed and halved
130 g (4½ oz) olives

Heat the oil in a large flameproof casserole and fry the onion for a minute or two. Add the garlic and the chicken and fry for as long as it takes to brown the chicken all over.

Add the tomato paste and white wine, along with the sugar, and stir everything together. Add the tomato and any juices, the parsley and the beans and bring to the boil. Turn down the heat, season well and simmer for 40 minutes.

Add the olives and simmer for another 5 minutes. The sauce should be thick by now and the chicken fully cooked. Add more salt and pepper, if necessary. Serve with potatoes, pasta or rice.

Serves 4

Salsicce with white beans and gremolata

3 tablespoons olive oil
12 salsicce or thick pork sausages,
    cut into chunks
6 garlic cloves, smashed
240 g (9 oz) chargrilled red or yellow
    capsicum (pepper)
2 x 400 g (14 oz) cans cannellini
    beans, drained and rinsed
1½ tablespoons grated lemon zest
6 tablespoons parsley, chopped
2 tablespoons lemon juice
extra virgin olive oil, for drizzling

Heat the olive oil in a frying pan and cook the salsicce until they are browned all over and cooked through. Lift them out of the frying pan with a slotted spoon and put them to one side.

Put 3 garlic cloves in the frying pan and cook them over a gentle heat until they are very soft. Cut the capsicum into strips and add them to the pan, along with the beans and salsicce. Stir together and cook over a gentle heat for 2 minutes to heat the salsicce through. Season well with salt and pepper.

To make the gremolata, smash the remaining 3 garlic cloves to a paste, with a little salt, in a mortar and pestle. Mix in the lemon zest and the chopped parsley and season with salt and pepper.

Just before serving, stir the gremolata through the beans and then finish the dish with the lemon juice and a drizzle of olive oil.

Serves 4

Stir-fried tofu with oyster sauce

500 g (1 lb 2 oz) firm tofu
3–4 tablespoons oil
2 garlic cloves, crushed
2 teaspoons grated ginger
2 tablespoons oyster sauce
2 tablespoons soy sauce
2 teaspoons sugar
8 oyster mushrooms, quartered
2 spring onions (scallions), cut into
    pieces
2 baby bok choy (pak choi), quartered
a large handful coriander (cilantro)
    leaves

Cut the tofu into bite-sized pieces. Heat a wok over a medium heat, add half the oil and heat until it is very hot and almost smoking. Cook half the tofu until golden brown on all sides, making sure you move it around gently or it will stick and break. Remove from the pan and repeat with the remaining oil and tofu. Return the tofu to the pan.

Add the garlic, ginger, oyster sauce, soy sauce and sugar, then toss until well combined. Add the oyster mushrooms, spring onion and bok choy, then simmer until the sauce has reduced a little and the spring onion and bok choy have softened slightly. Garnish with the coriander leaves.

Serves 4

Chive gnocchi with blue cheese

900 g (2 lb) floury potatoes
330 g (2²/₃ cups) plain (all-purpose) flour
2 tablespoons chives, chopped
4 egg yolks
90 g (3¹/₄ oz) blue cheese
160 ml (²/₃ cup) cream

Peel the potatoes and cut them into even-sized pieces. Cook them in simmering water for 20 minutes, or until they are tender. Drain them very well, then mash them in a large bowl. Add 280 g (10 oz) of the flour, the chives and egg yolks, along with some seasoning, and mix well. Now add enough of the remaining flour to make a mixture that is soft but not sticky. Divide the mixture into four, roll each bit into a sausage shape 1 cm (¹/₂ in) across and cut off lengths about 1.5 cm (⁵/₈ in) long. You don't need to shape the gnocchi any more than this.

Bring a large saucepan of water to the boil and cook the gnocchi in batches. As it rises to the surface (it will do this when it is cooked through), scoop it out with a slotted spoon and drain well.

While the gnocchi are cooking, put the blue cheese and cream in a saucepan and gently heat them together. Put the gnocchi in a large bowl and pour the blue cheese sauce over it. Gently fold the sauce into the gnocchi and serve.

Serves 4

Pastitsio

2 tablespoons oil
4 garlic cloves, crushed
2 onions, chopped
1 kg (2 lb 4 oz) minced (ground) beef
1 kg (2 lb 4 oz) canned peeled
   tomatoes, chopped
250 ml (1 cup) dry red wine
250 ml (1 cup) beef stock
1 bay leaf
1 teaspoon dried mixed herbs
350 g (12 oz) ziti pasta
3 eggs, lightly beaten
500 g (1 lb 2 oz) Greek-style yoghurt
200 g (7 oz) kefalotyri cheese, grated
1/2 teaspoon ground nutmeg
60 g (1/2 cup) grated Cheddar cheese
oakleaf lettuce, to serve

Heat the oil in a large heavy-based
pan, and cook the garlic and onion
over medium heat for 5 minutes,
or until the onion is soft. Add the
beef and cook over high heat until
browned, then drain off any excess
fat. Add the tomato, wine, stock, bay
leaf and herbs and bring to the boil.
Reduce the heat and simmer for
40 minutes. Season well.

Preheat the oven to 180°C (350°F/
Gas 4). Meanwhile, cook the pasta in
a large pan of rapidly boiling water
until *al dente*. Drain well and spread in
the base of a large ovenproof dish.
Pour in half the egg and top with
the sauce.

Combine the yoghurt, remaining egg,
kefalotyri and nutmeg and pour over
the top. Sprinkle with the Cheddar
and bake for 40 minutes, or until
golden brown. Leave to stand for
10 minutes before serving with
oakleaf lettuce.

Serves 6–8

Spinach and ricotta ravioli

1 tablespoon olive oil
1 red onion, finely chopped
1 garlic clove, crushed
200 g (about 6 handfuls) baby English
  spinach leaves, coarsely chopped
250 g (1 cup) ricotta cheese
2 egg yolks, beaten
2 tablespoons grated Parmesan
  cheese
freshly grated nutmeg
48 won ton wrappers
2 tablespoons butter
2 tablespoons sage leaves

Heat the oil in a frying pan, add the onion and garlic and fry them over a low heat for a few minutes until the onion goes soft and translucent. Add the spinach and stir it around until it wilts.

Stir the spinach mixture into the ricotta, along with the egg yolk, Parmesan, some nutmeg and some salt and pepper.

Brush a little water around the edge of a won ton wrapper and put a teaspoon of filling in the centre. Fold the wrapper over to make a half moon shape and press the edges firmly together. Put the ravioli on a tea towel laid out on your work surface and repeat with the remaining wrappers.

Bring a large saucepan of water to the boil and cook the ravioli for a few minutes. They will float to the surface when they are ready. Scoop them out carefully with a slotted spoon and drain them in a colander. Melt the butter in a small saucepan, add the sage and sizzle for a few minutes until the butter browns slightly. Put the ravioli in bowls and pour the butter and sage over them.

Serves 4

Egg fried rice

4 eggs
1 spring onion (scallion), chopped
50 g (1/3 cup) fresh or frozen peas
  (optional)
3 tablespoons oil
740 g (4 cups) cooked long-grain rice

Beat the eggs with a pinch of salt and 1 teaspoon of the spring onion. Cook the peas in a pan of simmering water for 3 minutes if fresh or 1 minute if frozen.

Heat a wok over high heat, add the oil and heat until very hot. Reduce the heat, add the egg and lightly scramble. Add the rice before the egg is completely set. Increase the heat, then stir to separate the rice grains and break the egg into small bits. Add the peas and the remaining spring onion, and season with salt. Stir constantly for 1 minute.

Serves 4

Grilled nachos

2 x 300 g (10½ oz) packets corn
  chips
4 tomatoes, chopped
1 red onion, finely chopped
3 jalapeño chillies, thinly sliced
2 tablespoons lime juice
4 tablespoons chopped coriander
  (cilantro) leaves
220 g (1½ cups) feta cheese,
  crumbled

Turn on the grill (broiler). Arrange the corn chips on four ovenproof plates.

Scatter the tomato, onion and chilli on top of the corn chips, then drizzle with the lime juice and season with some salt. Scatter the coriander and feta cheese over the top, making sure the corn chips are well covered.

Grill the nachos until they start to brown around the edges and the cheese starts to melt. Serve hot but be careful of the plates — they will be very hot too.

Serves 4

Ramen noodle soup with char siu

300 g (8 nests) dried thin ramen egg
noodles
1 litre (4 cups) chicken stock
4 spring onions (scallions), shredded
4 tablespoons soy sauce
400 g (5 cm/2 in long piece) char siu
2 small bok choy (pak choi), roughly
chopped
sesame oil, for drizzling

Cook the noodles in a large saucepan of boiling salted water for about 4 minutes, or until they are just cooked, stirring once or twice to make sure they are not stuck together. The cooking time will vary depending on the brand of noodles.

Bring the chicken stock to the boil in a saucepan, then add the spring onion and soy sauce. Taste the stock to see if it has enough flavour and, if not, add a bit more soy sauce — don't overdo it though as the soup's base should be quite mild in flavour. Turn the heat down to a simmer. Cut the char siu into bite-sized shreds or slices (small enough to pick up and eat with chopsticks).

Drain the noodles and divide them among four bowls. Add the bok choy to the chicken stock, stir it in, then divide the stock and vegetables among the four bowls. Arrange the char siu on top, then drizzle a little sesame oil onto each — sesame oil has a very strong flavour, so you will only need a couple of drops for each bowl.

Serves 4

Hot and sweet chicken

125 ml (1/2 cup) rice vinegar

160 g (2/3 cup) caster (superfine) sugar

6 garlic cloves, crushed

a large pinch of chilli flakes

1 teaspoon ground coriander

1 teaspoon ground white pepper

2 bunches coriander (cilantro), finely chopped, including roots and stems

3 tablespoons olive oil

2 tablespoons lemon juice

8 boneless and skinless chicken thighs, cut in half

2 tablespoons caster (superfine) sugar, extra

2 tablespoons fish sauce

1 small cucumber, peeled and sliced

Put the vinegar and sugar in a small saucepan, bring to the boil, then turn down the heat and simmer for a minute. Take the mixture off the heat and add two crushed garlic cloves, the chilli flakes and a pinch of salt. Leave the dressing to cool.

Heat a small frying pan for a minute, add the ground coriander and white pepper and stir it around for a minute. This will make the spices more fragrant. Add the rest of the garlic, the fresh coriander and a pinch of salt. Add 2 tablespoons of the oil and all the lemon juice and mix to a paste. Rub this all over the chicken pieces.

Heat the rest of the oil in a wok, add the chicken and fry it on both sides for 8 minutes, or until it is cooked through. Sprinkle in the extra sugar and the fish sauce and cook for another minute or two until any excess liquid has evaporated and the chicken pieces are sticky. Serve the chicken with the sliced cucumber and some rice. Dress with the sauce.

Serves 4

Lamb pilaff

1 large eggplant (aubergine), cut into
   1 cm (½ in) cubes
125 ml (½ cup) olive oil
1 large onion, finely chopped
1 teaspoon ground cinnamon
2 teaspoons ground cumin
1 teaspoon ground coriander
300 g (1½ cups) long-grain rice
500 ml (2 cups) chicken or vegetable
   stock
500 g (1 lb 2 oz) minced (ground)
   lamb
½ teaspoon allspice
2 tablespoons olive oil, extra
2 tomatoes, cut into wedges
3 tablespoons toasted pistachios
2 tablespoons currants
2 tablespoons chopped coriander
   (cilantro) leaves, to garnish

Put the eggplant in a colander, sprinkle with salt and leave for 1 hour. Rinse and squeeze dry. Heat 2 tablespoons of the oil in a large, deep frying pan with a lid, add the eggplant and cook over medium heat for 8–10 minutes. Drain on paper towels.

Heat the remaining oil, add the onion and cook for 4–5 minutes, or until soft. Stir in half each of the cinnamon, cumin and ground coriander. Add the rice and stir to coat, then add the stock, season and bring to the boil. Reduce the heat and simmer, covered, for 15 minutes.

Put the lamb in a bowl with the allspice and remaining cumin, cinnamon and ground coriander. Season with salt and pepper, and mix. Roll into balls the size of macadamia nuts. Heat the extra oil in the frying pan and cook the meatballs in batches over medium heat for 5 minutes each batch. Drain on paper towels.

Add the tomato to the pan and cook, for 3–5 minutes, or until golden. Remove from the pan. Stir the eggplant, pistachios, currants and meatballs through the rice. Serve the pilaff with the tomato and coriander.

Serves 4

Saffron chicken and rice

60 ml (¼ cup) olive oil
4 chicken thighs and 6 drumsticks
1 large red onion, finely chopped
1 large green capsicum (pepper),
   two-thirds diced and one-third
   julienned
3 teaspoons sweet paprika
400 g (14 oz) can chopped tomatoes
250 g (1¼ cups) long-grain rice
½ teaspoon ground saffron

Heat 2 tablespoons of the oil in a deep frying pan over high heat. Season the chicken pieces well and brown in batches. Remove the chicken from the pan.

Reduce the heat to medium and add the remaining oil. Add the onion and diced capsicum, and cook gently for 5 minutes. Stir in the paprika and cook for about 30 seconds. Add the tomato and simmer for 1–3 minutes, or until the mixture thickens.

Stir 875 ml (3½ cups) of boiling water into the pan, then add the rice and saffron. Return the chicken to the pan and stir to combine. Season with salt and pepper. Bring to the boil, cover, reduce the heat to medium–low and simmer for 20 minutes, or until all the liquid has been absorbed and the chicken is tender. Stir in the julienned capsicum, then allow it to stand, covered, for 3–4 minutes before serving.

Serves 4

Porcini and walnut pasta

20 g (½ oz) or 2 small packets porcini
400 g (14 oz) penne
2 tablespoons olive oil
1 onion, finely chopped
2 garlic cloves, crushed
24 button mushrooms, sliced
3 thyme sprigs
90 g (3¼ oz) walnuts
2 tablespoons sour cream
Parmesan cheese, grated

Put the porcini in a bowl with just enough boiling water to cover them and leave to soak for half an hour. If they soak up all the water quickly, add a little more.

Cook the penne in a large saucepan of boiling salted water until it is *al dente*, stirring once or twice to make sure the pieces are not stuck together. The cooking time will vary, depending on the brand of pasta. Check the pasta occasionally as it cooks because packet instructions are often too long by a minute or two.

Heat the oil in a deep frying pan and fry the onion and garlic together until translucent but not browned. Add the porcini and any soaking liquid, mushrooms and thyme, and keep frying. The mushrooms will give off liquid as they cook so keep cooking until they soak it back up again.

In a separate pan, fry the walnuts without any oil until they start to brown and smell toasted. When they have cooled down a bit, roughly chop and add them to the frying pan. Toss with the drained penne, stir the sour cream through and season well. Serve with the Parmesan.

Serves 4

Classic jambalaya

2 tablespoons olive oil
1 large red onion, finely chopped
1 garlic clove, crushed
2 back bacon rashers, finely chopped
300 g (1½ cups) long-grain rice
1 red capsicum (pepper), diced
150 g (5½ oz) ham, chopped
400 g (14 oz) can chopped tomatoes
400 g (14 oz) tomato passata or
  tomato pasta sauce
1 teaspoon Worcestershire sauce
dash of Tabasco sauce
½ teaspoon dried thyme
30 g (½ cup) chopped parsley
150 g (5½ oz) cooked, peeled, small
  prawns (shrimp)
4 spring onions (scallions), thinly
  sliced

Heat the oil in a large saucepan over medium heat. Add the onion, garlic and bacon and cook, stirring, for 5 minutes, or until the onion is softened but not browned. Stir in the rice and cook for a further 5 minutes, or until lightly golden.

Add the capsicum, ham, tomatoes, tomato passata, Worcestershire and Tabasco sauces and thyme and stir until well combined. Bring the mixture to the boil, then reduce the heat to low. Cook, covered, for 30–40 minutes, or until the rice is tender.

Stir in the parsley and prawns and season with salt and freshly ground black pepper. Sprinkle with the spring onion, then serve.

Serves 4–6

Thai basil fried rice

2 tablespoons oil
3 Asian shallots, sliced
1 garlic clove, finely chopped
1 small red chilli, finely chopped
100 g (3½ oz) snake or green beans,
  cut into short pieces
1 small red capsicum (pepper), cut
  into batons
90 g (3¼ oz) button mushrooms,
  halved
470 g (2½ cups) cooked jasmine rice
1 teaspoon grated palm sugar
3 tablespoons light soy sauce
10 g (¼ cup) fresh Thai basil,
  shredded
1 tablespoon coriander (cilantro)
  leaves, chopped
fried red Asian shallot flakes,
  to garnish
Thai basil leaves, to garnish

Heat a wok over high heat, add the oil
and swirl. Stir-fry the shallots, garlic
and chilli for 3 minutes, or until the
shallots start to brown. Add the
beans, capsicum and mushrooms,
stir-fry for 3 minutes, or until cooked,
then stir in the cooked jasmine rice
and heat through.

Dissolve the palm sugar in the soy
sauce, then pour over the rice. Stir
in the herbs. Garnish with the shallot
flakes and basil.

Serves 4

Roast vegetables with poached egg and camembert

12 baby onions or French shallots
80 ml (1/3 cup) olive oil
2 bundles asparagus, cut into 4 cm
  (1 1/2 in) pieces
4 zucchini (courgettes), thickly sliced
2 eggplants (aubergines), cubed
8 garlic cloves
2 tablespoons lemon juice
4 eggs
250 g (9 oz) Camembert cheese,
  cubed

Turn the oven on to 200°C (400°F/ Gas 6). Peel the baby onions, leaving them still attached at the root end. Don't leave any root on.

Put the oil in a roasting tin and add the onions, asparagus, zucchini and eggplant, along with the garlic, and toss well. Season with salt and black pepper. Put the tin in the oven and roast the vegetables for 20 minutes. Sprinkle on the lemon juice and roast for another 10 minutes.

Put a large frying pan full of water over a high heat and bring it to the boil. When the water is bubbling, turn the heat down to a gentle simmer. Crack an egg into a cup and slip the egg into the water — it should start to turn opaque. Do the same with the other egg, keeping them separate. Turn the heat down as low as you can and leave the eggs for 3 minutes.

Divide the vegetables between four ovenproof dishes. Put the Camembert on top of the vegetables, dividing it among the dishes. Put the dishes back in the oven for a couple of minutes to start the cheese melting.

Top each dish with a poached egg and some black pepper.

Serves 4

Chilli linguine with chermoula chicken

600 g (1 lb 5 oz) chicken breast fillets
500 g (1 lb 2 oz) chilli linguine

Chermoula
100 g (2 cups) coriander (cilantro),
  leaves, chopped
60 g (2 cups) flat-leaf (Italian) parsley
  leaves, chopped
4 garlic cloves, crushed
2 teaspoons ground cumin
2 teaspoons ground paprika
125 ml (½ cup) lemon juice
2 teaspoons lemon zest
100 ml (3½ fl oz) olive oil

Heat a large non-stick frying pan over medium heat. Add the chicken breasts and cook until tender. Remove from the pan and leave for 5 minutes before cutting into thin slices.

Cook the pasta in a large saucepan of rapidly boiling salted water until *al dente*, then drain.

Meanwhile, combine the chermoula ingredients in a glass bowl and add the sliced chicken. Leave to stand until the pasta has finished cooking. Serve the pasta topped with the chermoula chicken.

Serves 4

Green chicken curry

250 ml (1 cup) coconut cream
4 tablespoons green curry paste
8 skinless chicken thighs or 4 chicken
    breasts, cut into pieces
250 ml (1 cup) coconut milk
4 Thai eggplants or ½ of a purple
    eggplant (aubergine), cut
    into chunks
2 tablespoons shaved palm sugar or
    brown sugar
2 tablespoons fish sauce
4 makrut (kaffir) lime leaves, torn
a handful Thai basil leaves
1–2 large red chillies, sliced
coconut milk or cream, for drizzling

Put a wok over a low heat, add the coconut cream and let it come to the boil. Stir it for a while until the oil separates out. Don't let it burn.

Add the green curry paste, stir for a minute, then add the chicken. Cook the chicken until it turns opaque, then add the coconut milk and eggplant. Cook for a minute or two until the eggplant is tender. Add the sugar, fish sauce, lime leaves and half of the basil, then mix together.

Garnish with the rest of the basil, the chilli and a drizzle of coconut milk or cream. Serve with rice.

Serves 4

Beef ball and white bean soup

600 g (1 lb 5 oz) minced (ground) beef
2 garlic cloves, crushed
1 tablespoon parsley, finely chopped
a large pinch ground cinnamon
a large pinch freshly grated nutmeg
2 eggs, lightly beaten
1.5 litres (6 cups) beef stock
2 carrots, thinly sliced
2 x 400 g (14 oz) cans white beans, drained
½ savoy cabbage, finely shredded
Parmesan cheese, grated

Put the beef in a bowl with the garlic, parsley, cinnamon, nutmeg and half of the egg. Mix everything together well and season with salt and pepper. If the mixture is dry, add the rest of the egg — you want it to be sticky enough so that forming small balls is easy.

Roll the beef mixture into small balls — they should be small enough to scoop up on a spoon and eat in one mouthful. Put them on a plate as you make them.

Put the beef stock in a saucepan, with the carrot, and bring it to the boil. Add the meatballs, one at a time, and turn the heat down to a simmer. Test one of the balls after 3 minutes. It should be cooked through, so if it isn't, cook them for a little longer. Now add the beans and cabbage and cook for another 4 to 5 minutes. Season the broth to taste.

Serve the soup with lots of Parmesan stirred in and plenty of bread to dunk into the broth.

Serves 4

Sweet and sour pork

600 g (1 lb 4 oz) pork loin, cubed
2 eggs
6 tablespoons cornflour (cornstarch)
1 tablespoon oil
1 onion, cubed
1 red capsicum (pepper), cubed
2 spring onions (scallions), cut
   into lengths
250 ml (1 cup) clear rice vinegar or
   white vinegar
80 ml (⅓ cup) tomato ketchup
220 g (1 cup) sugar
2 tablespoons oil, extra

Put the pork cubes and egg in a bowl with 4 tablespoons of the cornflour. Stir everything around to coat the pork well, then tip into a sieve and shake off any excess cornflour.

Heat a wok over a high heat, add a tablespoon of oil and heat it until it just starts to smoke. Add the onion and cook it for a minute. Add the red capsicum and spring onion and cook for another minute. Add the rice vinegar, tomato ketchup and sugar, turn down the heat and stir everything together until the sugar dissolves. Bring to the boil and simmer it for about 3 minutes.

Mix 2 tablespoons of cornflour with 2 tablespoons of water, add it to the sweet-and-sour mixture, then simmer for a minute until the sauce thickens a bit. Pour the sauce into a bowl.

Heat half the remaining oil in a non-stick frying pan over a medium heat. As soon as the oil is hot, slide in half the pork cubes into the pan and cook them until they are browned and crisp. Remove from pan. Repeat with remaining oil and pork. Return all the pork to the pan and add the sauce. Reheat everything until the sauce is bubbling.

Serves 4

Nasi goreng

2 eggs
80 ml (⅓ cup) oil
3 garlic cloves, finely chopped
1 onion, finely chopped
2 red chillies, seeded and very finely
    chopped
1 teaspoon shrimp paste
1 teaspoon coriander seeds
½ teaspoon sugar
400 g (14 oz) raw prawns (shrimp),
    peeled and deveined
200 g (7 oz) rump steak, finely sliced
200 g (1 cup) long-grain rice, cooked
    and cooled
2 teaspoons kecap manis
1 tablespoon soy sauce
4 spring onions (scallions), finely
    chopped
½ lettuce, finely shredded
1 cucumber, thinly sliced
3 tablespoons crisp fried onions

Beat the eggs and ¼ teaspoon of salt until foamy. Heat a frying pan and brush with a little oil. Pour about one-quarter of the mixture into the pan and cook for 1–2 minutes over medium heat, or until the omelette sets. Turn the omelette over and cook the other side for about 30 seconds. Remove the omelette from the pan and repeat with the remaining mixture. When the omelettes are cold, roll them up, cut into fine strips and set aside.

Combine the garlic, onion, chilli, shrimp paste, coriander and sugar in a food processor, and process until a paste is formed.

Heat 1–2 tablespoons of the oil in a wok; add the paste and cook over high heat for 1 minute. Add the prawns and steak, and stir-fry for 2–3 minutes.

Add the remaining oil and the cold rice to the wok. Stir-fry until the rice is heated through. Add the kecap manis, soy sauce and spring onion, and stir-fry for another minute.

Arrange the lettuce around the outside of a large platter. Put the rice in the centre, and garnish with the omelette, cucumber slices and crisp fried onion. Serve immediately.

Serves 4

Linguine with roasted cherry tomatoes

400 g (14 oz) linguine
500 g (1 lb 2 oz) red cherry tomatoes
500 g (1 lb 2 oz) yellow cherry
  tomatoes
2 tablespoons olive oil
2 garlic clove, crushed
4 spring onions (scallions), sliced
1 bunch chives, finely chopped
100 g (about 20) black olives
extra virgin olive oil, for drizzling

Cook the linguine in a large saucepan of boiling salted water until *al dente*, stirring once or twice to make sure the pieces are not stuck together. The cooking time will vary depending on the brand of linguine. Check the pasta occasionally as it cooks because the time given on packet instructions is often too long by a minute or two.

Cut all the cherry tomatoes in half. Heat the oil in a saucepan, add the garlic and spring onion and let them sizzle briefly. Tip in the cherry tomatoes and cook them over a high heat until they just start to collapse and give off their juices. Add the chives and olives, season with salt and pepper and toss everything together well.

Drain the linguine and put it in a large serving bowl or individual bowls. Pour the cherry tomato mixture on top and grind some black pepper over the top. Drizzle with a little bit more olive oil if you like.

Serves 4

Chilli

165 g (6 oz) black beans or kidney
 beans
3 tablespoons oil
1 red onion, finely chopped
2 garlic cloves, crushed
1½ bunches coriander (cilantro), finely
 chopped
2 chillies, seeded and finely chopped
1.2 kg (2 lb 10 oz) chuck steak, cut
 into cubes
600 g (1 lb 5 oz) canned chopped
 tomatoes
1½ tablespoons tomato paste (purée)
375 ml (1½ cups) beef stock
1½ red capsicums (peppers), cut
 into squares
1 large ripe tomato, chopped
1 avocado, diced
2 limes, juiced
4 tablespoons sour cream

Put the beans in a saucepan, cover with water, bring to the boil, then turn down the heat and simmer for 10 minutes. Turn off the heat and leave for 2 hours. Drain and rinse the beans.

Heat half of the oil in a large heatproof casserole dish. Cook three-quarters of the onion, garlic, half of the coriander, and the chilli, for 5 minutes.

Remove the onion from the casserole dish and set aside. Heat half the remaining oil in the dish, add half the steak and cook until well browned. Repeat with the remaining oil and steak. Return the onions and meat to the pan. Add the beans, tomato, tomato paste and stir together. Bring to the boil, then turn it down to a simmer. Put the lid on and cook it for 1 hour and 20 minutes. Add the red capsicum to the casserole, stir it in and cook for another 40 minutes.

To make the topping, mix half of the remaining coriander, tomato, avocado and onion. Season with salt and pepper and add half of the lime juice.

When the meat is tender, add the coriander and lime juice and season well. Serve with the topping spooned over and a dollop of sour cream.

Serves 4

Lamb curry

1 kg (2 lb 4 oz) lamb leg or shoulder,
  cubed
80 ml (⅓ cup) thick plain yoghurt
2 onions, chopped
2 green chillies, roughly chopped
2 garlic cloves, crushed
2 cm (¾ in) piece ginger, grated
50 g (⅓ cup) cashews
4 tablespoons korma curry paste
2 tablespoons oil

Put the lamb in a bowl with half the yoghurt and mix together until all the meat cubes are coated.

Put the onion with the chilli, garlic, ginger, cashew nuts and curry paste in a blender, add 80 ml (⅓ cup) of water and process to a smooth paste. If you don't have a blender, finely chop everything before adding the water.

Heat the oil in a casserole dish over a medium heat. Add the blended mixture, season with salt and cook over a low heat for 1 minute, or until the liquid evaporates and the sauce thickens. Add the lamb and slowly bring everything to the boil. Cover the casserole tightly, simmer for 1 hour and 15 minutes, then add the rest of the yoghurt and keep cooking for another 30 minutes, or until the meat is very tender. Stir the meat occasionally to prevent it from sticking to the pan. The sauce should be quite thick. Serve with rice.

Serves 4

Grilled chicken with capsicum couscous

200 g (1 cup) instant couscous
1 tablespoon olive oil
1 onion, finely chopped
2 zucchini (courgettes), sliced
½ red or yellow chargrilled capsicum (pepper), chopped
12 semi-dried (sun-blushed) tomatoes, chopped
½ tablespoon grated orange zest
250 ml (1 cup) orange juice
a large handful chopped mint
8 chicken thighs or 4 chicken breasts, skin on
2 tablespoons butter, softened

Heat the grill (broiler). Bring 500 ml (2 cups) water to the boil in a saucepan, throw in the couscous, then take the pan off the heat and leave it to stand for 10 minutes.

Heat the oil in a frying pan and fry the onion and zucchini until lightly browned. Add the capsicum and semi-dried tomatoes, then stir in the couscous. Stir in the orange zest, one-third of the orange juice and the mint.

Put the chicken in a large shallow baking dish in a single layer and dot it with the butter. Sprinkle with the remaining orange juice and season well with salt and pepper. Grill the chicken for 8 to 10 minutes, turning it over halfway through. The skin should be browned and crisp.

Serve the chicken on the couscous with any juices poured over it.

Serves 4

Shepherd's pie

1 tablespoon oil
1 onion, finely chopped
1 carrot, finely chopped
1 kg (2 lb 4 oz) minced (ground) lamb,
   raw or cooked
plain (all-purpose) flour, for thickening
2 tablespoons tomato ketchup
2 beef stock cubes
Worcestershire sauce
6 potatoes, cut into chunks
80 ml (1/3 cup) milk
butter

Turn the oven on to 200°C (400°F/ Gas 6). Heat the oil in a frying pan, add the onion and carrot and fry them together until they begin to brown around the edges. Add the meat and cook, turning over every now and then, mashing out any large lumps with the back of a fork.

When the meat is browned all over, add a little flour, about a teaspoon, and stir it in. Add the ketchup and sprinkle on the stock cube. Now add about 500 ml (2 cups) of water and mix everything together. Bring the mixture to the boil, then turn down the heat and simmer gently for about 30 minutes, or until thick. Season with salt, pepper and Worcestershire sauce.

While the meat is cooking, cook the potato chunks in simmering water until they are tender (this will take about 12 minutes). When they are soft, drain and mash them with the milk and plenty of seasoning. Pour the meat into a large ovenproof dish or four individual dishes and dollop the potato on top. Dot some butter over the potato and bake for about 20 minutes, by which time the top of the potato should be lightly browned. Serve with peas.

Serves 4

Goan prawn curry

1 tablespoon oil
2 tablespoons curry paste
1 onion, finely chopped
2 tomatoes, chopped
3 garlic cloves, chopped
2 green chillies, finely chopped
2 cm (½ in) piece ginger, grated
2 tablespoons tamarind purée
80 ml (⅓ cup) coconut cream
500 g (about 20) prawns (shrimp),
 peeled and deveined

Heat the oil in a deep frying pan and fry the curry paste for about a minute, by which time it should start to be aromatic. Add the onion and fry until it is golden. Add the tomato, garlic, green chilli and ginger and fry over a low heat, stirring occasionally, for about 10 minutes, or until the oil separates out from the sauce.

Add the tamarind to the pan and bring everything to the boil. Add the coconut cream and stir. Season with salt.

Add the prawns and bring everything slowly to the boil. (The sauce is not very liquidy, but it needs to be made very hot in order to cook the prawns.) Simmer the prawns for 3–5 minutes, or until they turn bright pink all over. Stir them around as they cook. Serve with rice or Indian breads.

Serves 4

Pulao with fried onions and spiced chicken

1 litre (4 cups) chicken stock
4 tablespoons oil
6 cardamom pods
2 x 5 cm (2 in) piece cinnamon stick
3 cloves
8 black peppercorns
270 g (1⅓ cups) basmati rice
2 handfuls coriander (cilantro) leaves
1 large onion, finely sliced
2 teaspoons curry paste (any type)
1 tablespoon tomato paste (purée)
2 tablespoons yoghurt
400 g (about 2) skinless chicken
  breast fillets, cut into strips
thick natural yoghurt, to serve
mango chutney, to serve

Heat the chicken stock in a small saucepan until it is simmering. Heat 1 tablespoon of the oil over a medium heat in a large heavy-based saucepan. Add the cardamom pods, cinnamon stick, cloves and peppercorns and fry for a minute. Reduce the heat to low, add the rice and stir constantly for 1 minute. Add the heated stock and some salt to the rice and quickly bring everything to the boil. Cover the saucepan and simmer the rice over a low heat for 15 minutes. Leave the rice to stand for 10 minutes, then stir in the coriander.

Heat 2 tablespoons of the oil in a frying pan and fry the onion until it is very soft. Increase the heat and keep frying until the onion turns dark brown. Drain the onion on paper towels, then add it to the rice.

Mix the curry paste, tomato paste and yoghurt together, then mix the paste thoroughly with the chicken strips.

Heat the remaining oil in a frying pan. Cook the chicken for about 4 minutes over a high heat until almost black in patches.

Serve the rice with the chicken strips, yoghurt and mango chutney.

Serves 4

Roast chicken pieces with herbed cheese

150 g (5½ oz) herbed cream cheese
1 teaspoon grated lemon zest
4 whole chicken legs (Marylands) or
  breasts, skin on
2 leeks, cut into chunks
2 parsnips, cut into chunks
2 teaspoons olive oil

Put the oven on to 200°C (400°F/ Gas 6). Mix the cream cheese with the lemon zest. Loosen the skin from the whole legs or chicken breasts and spread 2 tablespoons of the cream cheese between the skin and flesh on each. Press the skin back down and season it.

Bring a saucepan of water to the boil and cook the leek and parsnip for 4 minutes. Drain them well and put them in a single layer in a baking dish. Drizzle with the oil and season well. Put the chicken on top and put the dish in the oven.

Roast for 40 minutes, by which time the skin should be browned and the cream cheese should have mostly melted out to form a sauce over the vegetables. Check that the vegetables are cooked and tender by prodding them with a knife. If they need a little longer, cover the dish with foil and cook for another 5 minutes. Keep the chicken warm under foil in the meantime.

Serves 4

Farfalle with prawns and lemon horseradish cream

400 g (14 oz) farfalle
1 tablespoon olive oil
2 French shallots, sliced
800 g (about 32) tiger prawns
  (shrimp), peeled and deveined
2 tablespoons lemon juice
6 tablespoons cream
2 teaspoons grated lemon zest
2 tablespoons horseradish cream
2 tablespoons chervil leaves

Cook the farfalle in a large saucepan of boiling salted water until *al dente*, stirring once or twice to make sure the pieces are not stuck together. The cooking time will vary depending on the brand of pasta. Check the pasta occasionally as it cooks because the time given on packet instructions is often too long by a minute or two.

Heat the oil in a frying pan and add the shallot. Cook for a minute, then add the prawns. Cook over a high heat for 2 or 3 minutes, or until the prawns have turned bright pink and are cooked through. Add the lemon juice and toss well. Turn off the heat and leave everything in the pan.

Put the cream in a glass bowl and whisk it until it just starts to thicken. Don't make it too thick because when you add the lemon zest and lemony prawns the acid will thicken it further. Fold the lemon zest, horseradish cream and chervil into the cream.

Drain the farfalle and tip it into a large bowl. Add the prawns and any lemon juice to the bowl, then add the cream mixture. Fold everything together and season with salt and pepper.

Serves 4

Spaghetti bolognese

2 tablespoons olive oil
2 garlic cloves, crushed
1 large onion, chopped
1 carrot, finely chopped
1 celery stalk, finely chopped
500 g (1 lb 2 oz) lean minced (ground) beef
500 ml (2 cups) beef stock
375 ml (1½ cups) red wine
2 x 425 g (15 oz) cans chopped tomatoes
1 teaspoon sugar
3 tablespoons finely chopped parsley
500 g (1 lb 2 oz) spaghetti
grated Parmesan cheese, to serve

Heat some olive oil in a large, deep frying pan, then add the garlic, onion, carrot and celery and stir over low heat for 5 minutes until the vegetables are just starting to become tender.

Increase the heat before adding the beef. You'll need to stir the meat to break up any lumps — a wooden spoon is good for this. Once the meat is nicely browned, add the stock, wine, tomatoes, sugar and parsley. Bring to the boil, then reduce the heat and simmer for 1½ hours or thereabouts, stirring occasionally. Season with salt and freshly ground black pepper.

Shortly before serving, cook the spaghetti in a large saucepan of boiling, salted water until al dente. Drain and serve with the meat sauce and the Parmesan cheese.

Serves 4–6

Spicy eggplant spaghetti

300 g (10½ oz) spaghetti
125 ml (½ cup) extra virgin olive oil
2 red chillies, finely sliced
1 onion, finely chopped
3 garlic cloves, crushed
4 bacon rashers, chopped
400 g (14 oz) eggplant (aubergine),
   diced
2 tablespoons balsamic vinegar
2 tomatoes, chopped
3 tablespoons shredded basil

Cook the pasta in a large pan of rapidly boiling water until *al dente*, then drain.

Heat 1 tablespoon of the oil in a large, deep frying pan and cook the chilli, onion, garlic and bacon over medium heat for 5 minutes, or until the onion is golden and the bacon browned. Remove from the pan and set aside.

Add half the remaining oil to the pan and cook half the eggplant over high heat, tossing to brown on all sides. Remove and repeat with the remaining oil and eggplant. Return the bacon mixture and all the eggplant to the pan, add the vinegar, tomato and basil and cook until heated through. Season well.

Serve the spaghetti topped with the eggplant mixture.

Serves 4

Red beans and rice

210 g (1 cup) red kidney beans
2 tablespoons oil
1 onion, finely chopped
1 green capsicum (pepper), chopped
3 celery stalks, finely chopped
2 garlic cloves, crushed
225 g (8 oz) andouille or other spicy
    sausage, cut into pieces
2 ham hocks
2 bay leaves
200 g (1 cup) long-grain rice
5 spring onions (scallions), finely
    sliced, to garnish

Soak the red kidney beans overnight in cold water. Drain and put into a saucepan with enough cold water to cover the beans. Bring to the boil, then reduce the heat to a simmer.

Heat the oil in a frying pan and sauté the onion, capsicum, celery and garlic until soft. Add the sausage and sauté until it begins to brown around the edges.

Add the sautéed vegetables and sausage to the beans along with the ham and bay leaves. Bring to the boil, then reduce to a simmer and cook for 2½–3 hours, adding more water if necessary — the beans should be saucy but not too liquidy. When the beans are almost cooked, boil the rice in a separate saucepan until it is tender.

Top the cooked rice with the red kidney beans. Tear some meat off the ham hocks and add to each serving plate. Garnish with the sliced spring onions.

Serves 4

Spaghetti with meatballs

Meatballs
500 g (1 lb 2 oz) minced (ground) beef
40 g (½ cup) fresh breadcrumbs
1 onion, finely chopped
2 garlic cloves, crushed
2 teaspoons Worcestershire sauce
1 teaspoon dried oregano
30 g (¼ cup) plain (all-purpose) flour
2 tablespoons olive oil

Sauce
2 x 400 g (14 oz) cans chopped
  tomatoes
1 tablespoon olive oil
1 onion, finely chopped
2 garlic cloves, crushed
2 tablespoons tomato paste (purée)
125 ml (½ cup) beef stock
2 teaspoons sugar

500 g (1 lb 2 oz) spaghetti
grated Parmesan cheese, optional

Combine the mince, breadcrumbs, onion, garlic, Worcestershire sauce and oregano in a bowl and season to taste. Use your hands to mix the ingredients together well. Roll level tablespoons of the mixture into balls, dust lightly with the flour and shake off the excess. Heat the oil in a deep frying pan and cook the meatballs in batches, turning frequently, until browned all over. Drain well.

To make the sauce, purée the tomatoes in a food processor or blender. Heat the oil in the cleaned frying pan. Add the onion and cook over medium heat for a few minutes until soft and just lightly golden. Add the garlic and cook for 1 minute more. Add the puréed tomatoes, tomato paste, stock and sugar to the pan and stir to combine. Bring the mixture to the boil, and add the meatballs. Reduce the heat and simmer for 15 minutes, turning the meatballs once. Season with salt and pepper.

Meanwhile, cook the spaghetti in a large pan of boiling water until just tender. Drain, divide among serving plates and top with the meatballs and sauce. Serve with grated Parmesan if desired.

Serves 4

Beef Stroganoff

500 g (1 lb 2 oz) rump steak
2 tablespoons plain (all-purpose) flour
2 tablespoons olive oil
1 onion, finely chopped
1 garlic clove, crushed
400 g (14 oz) button mushrooms,
  sliced
1 tablespoon tomato paste (purée)
300 g (10½ oz) sour cream
finely chopped parsley, to serve

Brandy (Splash)
paprika

Trim excess fat off the meat and slice it across the grain into thin pieces. Put the flour in a plastic bag and season well with salt and cracked black pepper. Add the steak and shake to coat the meat. Shake off any excess flour.

Heat 1 tablespoon oil in a large heavy-based frying pan over high heat. Add the meat and cook in batches until well browned. Remove from the pan and set aside.

Heat the remaining oil and add the onion. Cook for 2–3 minutes, or until soft and translucent, then add the garlic and stir briefly. Add the mushrooms and cook for about 3 minutes, or until soft. Stir in the tomato paste and sour cream, then add the beef strips. Stir until well combined and heated through. Sprinkle with chopped parsley before serving with rice.

Serves 4

Snapper pies

2 tablespoons olive oil
4 onions, thinly sliced
375 ml (1 1/2 cups) fish stock
875 ml (3 1/2 cups) cream
1 kg (2 lb 4 oz) skinless snapper
   fillets, cut into large pieces
2 sheets puff pastry, thawed
1 egg, lightly beaten

Preheat the oven to 220°C (425°F/ Gas 7). Heat the oil in a deep frying pan, add the onions and stir over a medium heat for 20 minutes, or until the onion is slightly caramelized. Add the fish stock, bring to the boil and cook for 10 minutes, or until the liquid is nearly evaporated. Stir in the cream and bring to the boil. Reduce the heat and simmer for 20 minutes, or until the liquid is reduced by half.

Divide half the sauce among four 500 ml (2 cup) capacity ramekins. Place some fish pieces in each ramekin and top with the remaining sauce. Cut the pastry sheets slightly larger than the tops of the ramekins. Brush the edges of the pastry with a little of the egg, press the pastry onto the ramekins and brush the pastry top with the remaining beaten egg. Bake for 30 minutes, or until well puffed.

Serves 4

Osso buco with gremolata

2 tablespoons olive oil
1 onion, finely chopped
1 garlic clove, crushed
1 kg (2 lb 4 oz) veal shin slices
  (osso buco)
2 tablespoons plain (all-purpose) flour
400 g (14 oz) can tomatoes, roughly
  chopped
250 ml (1 cup) white wine
250 ml (1 cup) chicken stock

Gremolata
2 tablespoons finely chopped parsley
2 teaspoons grated lemon zest
1 teaspoon finely chopped garlic

Heat 1 tablespoon oil in a large shallow flameproof casserole dish. Add the onion and cook over low heat until soft and golden. Add the garlic. Cook for 1 minute, then remove from the dish.

Heat the remaining oil and brown the veal in batches, then remove. Return the onion to the casserole and stir in the flour. Cook for 30 seconds and remove from the heat. Slowly stir in the tomatoes, wine and stock, combining well with the flour. Return the veal to the casserole.

Return to the heat and bring to the boil, stirring. Cover and reduce the heat to low so that the casserole is just simmering. Cook for $2\frac{1}{2}$ hours, or until the meat is very tender and almost falling off the bones.

To make the gremolata, combine the parsley, lemon zest and garlic in a bowl. When the osso buco is ready, sprinkle the gremolata over the top and serve with risotto or plain rice.

Serves 4

Note: Try to make this a day in advance as the flavours will improve considerably.

Asian chicken noodle soup

3 dried Chinese mushrooms
185 g (6½ oz) thin dry egg noodles
1 tablespoon oil
4 spring onions (scallions), julienned
1 tablespoon soy sauce
2 tablespoons rice wine, mirin or
    sherry
1.25 litres (5 cups) chicken stock
½ small barbecued chicken,
    shredded
50 g (1¾ oz) sliced ham, cut into
    strips
90 g (1 cup) bean sprouts
coriander (cilantro) leaves and thinly
    sliced red chilli, to garnish

Soak the mushrooms in boiling water for 10 minutes to soften them. Squeeze dry then remove the tough stem from the mushrooms and slice them thinly.

Cook the noodles in a large pan of boiling water for 3 minutes, or according to the manufacturer's directions. Drain and cut the noodles into shorter lengths with scissors.

Heat the oil in a large heavy-based pan. Add the mushrooms and spring onion. Cook for 1 minute, then add the soy sauce, rice wine and stock. Bring slowly to the boil and cook for 1 minute. Reduce the heat then add the noodles, shredded chicken, ham and bean sprouts. Heat through for 2 minutes without allowing to boil.

Use tongs to divide the noodles among four bowls, ladle in the remaining mixture, and garnish with coriander leaves and sliced chilli.

Serves 4

Genovese pesto sauce

Pesto
2 garlic cloves
50 g (1¾ oz) pine nuts
120 g (4½ oz) basil, stems removed
150–180 ml (5–6 fl oz) extra virgin
  olive oil
50 g (1¾ oz) Parmesan cheese, finely
  grated, plus extra to serve

500 g (1 lb 2 oz) trenette
175 g (6 oz) green beans, trimmed
175 g (6 oz) small potatoes, very
  thinly sliced

Put the garlic and pine nuts in a mortar and pestle or food processor and pound or process until finely ground. Add the basil and then drizzle in the olive oil a little at a time while pounding or processing. When you have a thick purée stop adding the oil. Season and mix in the Parmesan.

Bring a large saucepan of salted water to the boil. Add the pasta, green beans and potatoes, stirring well to prevent the pasta from sticking together. Cook until the pasta is *al dente* (the vegetables should be cooked by this time), then drain, reserving a little of the water.

Return the pasta and vegetables to the saucepan, add the pesto, and mix well. If necessary, add some of the reserved water to loosen the pasta. Season and serve immediately with the extra Parmesan.

Serves 4

Prawn pulao

200 g (1 cup) basmati rice
300 g (10½ oz) small prawns (shrimp)
3 tablespoons oil
1 onion, finely chopped
1 stick of cinnamon
6 cardamom pods
5 cloves
1 stalk lemon grass, finely chopped
4 garlic cloves, crushed
5 cm (2 in) piece of fresh ginger, grated
¼ teaspoon ground turmeric

Wash the rice under cold running water and drain. Peel and devein the prawns, then wash and pat dry with paper towels.

Heat the oil in a frying pan over a low heat and fry the onion, spices and lemon grass. Stir in the garlic, ginger and turmeric. Add the prawns and stir until pink. Toss in the rice and fry for 2 minutes. Pour in 500 ml (2 cups) of boiling water and add a pinch of salt. Bring to the boil. Reduce the heat and simmer for 15 minutes. Remove from the heat, cover and stand for 10 minutes. Fluff up the rice before serving.

Serves 4

Spicy Portuguese chicken soup

2.5 litres (10 cups) chicken stock
1 onion, cut into thin wedges
1 celery stalk, finely chopped
1 teaspoon grated lemon zest
3 tomatoes, peeled, seeded and
  chopped
1 sprig mint
1 tablespoon olive oil
2 chicken breast fillets
200 g (1 cup) long-grain rice
2 tablespoons lemon juice
2 tablespoons shredded mint

Combine the chicken stock, onion, celery, lemon zest, tomatoes, mint and olive oil in a large saucepan. Slowly bring to the boil, then reduce the heat, add the chicken and simmer gently for 20–25 minutes, or until the chicken is cooked through.

Remove the chicken from the saucepan and discard the mint sprig. Allow the chicken to cool, then thinly slice.

Meanwhile, add the rice to the pan and simmer for 25–30 minutes, or until the rice is tender. Return the sliced chicken to the pan, add the lemon juice and stir for 1–2 minutes, or until the chicken is warmed through. Season with salt and pepper, and stir through the mint.

Serves 6

Spiced eggplant

2 eggplants (aubergines), sliced
2 onions, finely chopped
2 cm (³/₄ in) piece fresh ginger, grated
4 garlic cloves, crushed
2 red chillies, finely chopped
500 g (2 cups) canned tomatoes
oil, for frying
½ teaspoon ground turmeric
½ teaspoon nigella seeds (kalonji)
2 teaspoons garam masala
a large handful coriander (cilantro),
  chopped

Put the eggplant slices in a colander, sprinkle them with salt and leave them for 30 minutes. Rinse the slices and squeeze them to get rid of any excess water, then pat them dry with paper towels.

Finely chop the tomatoes then mix the onion, ginger, garlic and chilli with the tomatoes.

Heat a little oil in a large, deep heavy-based frying pan and, when it is hot, add as many eggplant slices as you can fit in a single layer. Cook them over a medium heat until they are browned on both sides, then drain them to get rid of any excess oil. Cook the rest of the eggplant in batches, using as much oil as you need and draining off the excess.

Heat a tablespoon of oil in the frying pan, add the turmeric, kalonji and garam masala and stir for a few seconds, then add the tomato mixture. Cook, stirring for 5 minutes, or until the mixture thickens. Carefully add the cooked eggplant so the slices stay whole, cover the pan and cook gently for about 15 minutes. Season with salt to taste and stir the coriander through.

Serves 4

Fajitas

185 ml (³/₄ cup) olive oil
2 tablespoons lime juice
4 garlic cloves, chopped
3 red chillies, chopped
2 tablespoons tequila (optional)
1 kg (2 lb 4 oz) rump steak, thinly
  sliced into strips
1 red and yellow capsicum (pepper),
  thinly sliced
1 red onion, thinly sliced
8 flour tortillas
guacamole
shredded lettuce
diced tomato
sour cream

First make a marinade out of the oil, lime juice, garlic, chilli, tequila and some pepper. Add the meat, cover and marinate it for several hours or overnight, if you have time.

Drain the meat and toss it with the capsicum and onion. Around the time that you want to eat, wrap the tortillas in foil and warm them in a 150°C (300°F/Gas 2) oven for about 5 minutes. Cook the meat and vegetables in batches in a sizzling hot heavy-based frying pan until cooked, then scoop onto a serving plate and sit in the middle of the table with the tortillas, guacamole, shredded lettuce, diced tomato and sour cream. Let everyone assemble their own fajita.

Serves 4

Dinner

Twice-baked cheese soufflés

250 ml (1 cup) milk
3 black peppercorns
1 onion, cut in half and studded with
  2 cloves
1 bay leaf
60 g (2¼ oz) butter
60 g (½ cup) self-raising flour
2 eggs, separated
125 g (4½ oz) Gruyère cheese, grated
250 ml (1 cup) cream
50 g (½ cup) Parmesan cheese, finely
  grated

Preheat the oven to 180°C (350°F/ Gas 4). Lightly grease four 125 ml (½ cup) ramekins. Place the milk, peppercorns, onion and bay leaf in a saucepan and heat until nearly boiling. Remove from the heat and let it infuse for 10 minutes. Strain.

Melt the butter in a saucepan, add the flour and cook over a medium heat for 1 minute. Remove from the heat and gradually stir in the infused milk, then return to the heat and stir until the mixture boils and thickens. Simmer for 1 minute.

Transfer the mixture to a bowl and add the egg yolks and Gruyère cheese. Beat the egg whites until soft peaks form, then gently fold into the cheese sauce. Divide the mixture between the ramekins and place in a baking dish half-filled with hot water. Bake for 15 minutes. Remove from the baking dish, cool and refrigerate.

Preheat the oven to 200°C (400°F/ Gas 6), remove the soufflés from the ramekins and place onto ovenproof plates. Pour cream over the top and sprinkle with Parmesan. Bake for 20 minutes, or until puffed and golden. Serve with a salad.

Serves 4

Pork loin with pickled eggplant

2 x 500 g (1 lb 2 oz) piece (about
   10 cm/4 in long) pork loin fillet
2 tablespoons hoisin sauce
a large pinch five-spice powder
4 tablespoons oil
1 eggplant (aubergine), cut into
   wedges
2 tablespoons soy sauce
2 teaspoons sesame oil
2 tablespoons balsamic vinegar
1/4 teaspoon caster (superfine) sugar
2 bok choy (pak choi), cut into
   quarters

Put the pork in a dish and add the hoisin sauce, five-spice powder and a tablespoon of oil. Rub the mixture over the pork and set it to one side. Heat another 2 tablespoons of oil in a non-stick frying pan and add the eggplant. Fry it until it softens and starts to brown, then add the soy sauce, sesame oil, vinegar and sugar and toss everything together for a minute. Tip the eggplant out onto a plate and wipe out the frying pan.

Put the last tablespoon of oil in the frying pan and put it over a medium heat. Add the pork and fry it on all sides until it is browned and cooked through. The time this takes will depend on how thick your piece of pork is — when it is cooked, it will feel firm when pressed. Put the eggplant back in the pan to heat through.

Take out the pork and leave it to sit for a minute or two. Cook the bok choy in a saucepan with a little bit of boiling water for 1 minute, then drain well. Slice the pork into medallions and serve it with the pickled eggplant and bok choy.

Serves 4

Coq au vin

1 tablespoon olive oil
12 white baby onions, peeled
3 rindless bacon rashers, chopped
40 g (1 1/2 oz) butter
1.5 kg (3 lb 5 oz) chicken pieces
2 garlic cloves, crushed
375 ml (1 1/2 cups) dry red wine
2 tablespoons brandy
1 tablespoon chopped thyme
1 bay leaf
4 parsley stalks
250 g (9 oz) button mushrooms,
  halved
20 g (1/2 oz) butter, extra, softened
20 g (1/2 oz) plain (all-purpose) flour
chopped parsley, to serve

Preheat the oven to warm 170°C (325°F/Gas 3). Heat the oil in a large heavy-based frying pan and add the onions. Cook until browned, then add the bacon and cook until browned. Remove the bacon and onions and add the butter to the pan. When the butter is foaming add the chicken in a single layer and cook in batches until well browned. Transfer the chicken to an ovenproof dish, draining it of any fat, then add the onions and bacon.

Tip any excess fat out of the frying pan and add the garlic, wine, brandy, thyme, bay leaf and parsley stalks. Bring to the boil and pour over the chicken. Cook, covered, in the oven for 1 hour and 25 minutes, then add the mushrooms and cook for 30 minutes. Drain through a colander and reserve the liquid in a pan. Keep the chicken warm in the oven.

Mix the softened butter and flour together, bring the liquid in the pan to the boil and whisk in the flour and butter paste in two batches, then reduce the heat and simmer until the liquid thickens slightly. Remove the parsley stalks and bay leaf from the chicken and return it to the ovenproof dish. Pour in the sauce, scatter on the chopped parsley and serve.

Serves 4

Beef Wellington

1.25 kg (2 lb 12 oz) piece of beef fillet
  or rib eye, trimmed
1 tablespoon oil
125 g (4½ oz) pâté
60 g (2¼ oz) button mushrooms,
  sliced
375 g (13 oz) block of puff pastry,
  thawed
1 egg, lightly beaten
1 sheet puff pastry, thawed
green beans, to serve
rosemary, to garnish

To help the beef keep its shape, tie it four or five times along its length, then rub with pepper. Heat the oil over high heat in a large, heavy-based pan, then cook the meat until it is browned all over. Take the beef out of the pan and let it cool, then cut off the string. Smear the pâté over the top and sides of the beef, then use this as glue to stick the mushrooms on.

The idea is to enclose the beef in puff pastry. Start by rolling the block of pastry out on a lightly floured surface until it is big enough. Then sit the beef on the pastry, brush the edges with egg and bring the edges up until you have a parcel of beef. Use some more of the beaten egg to seal the parcel, then neatly fold in the ends. Lift the beef onto a greased baking tray so the seam is underneath.

Cut shapes from the sheet of pastry. Use the egg to stick the shapes on, then brush all over the Wellington with more of the egg. Cut a few slits in the top to allow the steam to escape. Cook in a 210°C (415°F/Gas 6–7) oven for 45 minutes for rare, 1 hour for medium or 1½ hours for well done. Rest for 10 minutes, then slice and serve. Serve with green beans and garnish with rosemary.

Serves 6–8

Swordfish with anchovy and caper sauce

Sauce

1 large garlic clove
1 tablespoon capers, rinsed and finely chopped
50 g (1³/₄ oz) anchovy fillets, finely chopped
1 tablespoon finely chopped rosemary or dried oregano
finely grated zest and juice of
¹/₂ lemon
4 tablespoons extra virgin olive oil
1 large tomato, finely chopped

4 swordfish steaks
1 tablespoon extra virgin olive oil
crusty Italian bread, to serve

Put the garlic in a mortar and pestle with a little salt and crush it. To make the sauce, mix together the garlic, capers, anchovies, rosemary or oregano, lemon zest and juice, oil and tomato. Leave for 10 minutes.

Preheat a griddle or grill (broiler) to very hot. Using paper towels, pat the swordfish dry and lightly brush with the olive oil. Season with salt and pepper. Sear the swordfish over high heat for about 2 minutes on each side (depending on the thickness of the steaks), or until just cooked. The best way to check if the fish is cooked is to pull apart the centre of one steak — the flesh should be opaque. (Serve with the cut side underneath.)

If the cooked swordfish is a little oily, drain it on paper towels, then place on serving plates and drizzle with the sauce. Serve with Italian bread to mop up the sauce.

Serves 4

Pepper steak

4 x 200 g (7 oz) fillet steaks
2 tablespoons oil
6 tablespoons black peppercorns,
  crushed
40 g (1½ oz) butter
3 tablespoons Cognac or brandy
125 ml (½ cup) thick (double/heavy)
  cream
green salad, to serve

Rub the steaks on both sides with the oil and press the crushed peppercorns into the meat so they don't come off while you're frying. Melt the butter in a large frying pan and cook the steaks for 2–4 minutes on each side, depending on how you like your steak.

Now for the fun part: add the Cognac or brandy and flambé by lighting the pan with your gas flame or a match (stand well back when you do this and keep a pan lid handy for emergencies). Lift the steaks out onto a warm plate. Add the wine to the pan and boil, stirring, for 1 minute to deglaze the pan. Add the cream and stir for a couple of minutes. Season with salt and pepper and pour over the steaks. Serve with green salad.

Serves 4

Teppanyaki

350 g (12 oz) fillet steak
assorted vegetables, such as green
  beans, slender eggplant (aubergine),
  shiitake mushrooms, red or green
  capsicum (pepper), spring onions
  (scallions)
12 prawns (shrimp), peeled and
  deveined, with tails intact
3 tablespoons oil
soy sauce

First, you need to slice the meat very thinly. The secret to this is to partially freeze the meat (about 30 minutes should be enough), then slice it with a very sharp knife. Place the meat slices in a single layer on a large serving platter and season well with salt and pepper.

Cut the vegetables into long, thin strips, then arrange them in separate bundles on a plate. Arrange the prawns on a third plate.

The idea with teppanyaki is to cook the meal at the table on a very hot electric grill (griddle) or frying pan. Lightly brush the pan with the oil. Quickly fry about a quarter of the meat, searing on both sides, and then push it over to the edge of the pan while you cook about a quarter of the vegetables and the prawns. Serve a small portion of the meat and vegetables to the diners, who dip the food into soy sauce. Repeat the process with the remaining meat and vegetables, cooking in batches as extra helpings are required. Serve with rice.

Serves 4

Steak with green peppercorn sauce

4 x 200 g (7 oz) fillet steaks
30 g (1 oz) butter
2 teaspoons oil
250 ml (1 cup) beef stock
185 ml (¾ cup) whipping cream
2 teaspoons cornflour (cornstarch)
2 tablespoons green peppercorns in
  brine, rinsed and drained
2 tablespoons brandy
potato chips, to serve
rosemary, to garnish

First of all, bash the steaks with a meat mallet to 1.5 cm (⅝ inch) thick. Next, nick the edges of the steaks to prevent them from curling when they are cooking.

Heat the butter and oil in a large heavy-based frying pan over high heat. Fry the steaks for 2–4 minutes on each side, depending on how you like your steak. Transfer to a serving plate and cover with foil.

Now add the stock to the pan juices and stir over low heat until boiling. Combine the cream and cornflour, then pour the mixture into the pan and stir constantly until the sauce becomes smooth and thick — a few minutes will do the trick. Add the peppercorns and brandy and boil for 1 more minute before taking the pan off the heat. Spoon the sauce over the steaks. Serve with potato chips and garnish with rosemary.

Serves 4

Pork chops pizzaiola

4 pork chops
4 tablespoons olive oil
600 g (1 lb 5 oz) ripe tomatoes
3 garlic cloves, crushed
3 basil leaves, torn into pieces
1 teaspoon finely chopped parsley,
  to serve

Using scissors or a knife, cut the pork fat at 5 mm ($^1/_4$ in) intervals around the rind. Brush the chops with 1 tablespoon of the olive oil and season well.

Remove the stems from the tomatoes and score a cross in the bottom of each one. Blanch in boiling water for 30 seconds. Transfer to cold water, peel the skin away from the cross and chop the tomatoes.

Heat 2 tablespoons of the oil in a saucepan over low heat and add the garlic. Soften without browning for 1–2 minutes, then add the tomato and season. Increase the heat, bring to the boil and cook for 5 minutes until thick. Stir in the basil.

Heat the remaining oil in a large frying pan with a tight-fitting lid. Brown the chops in batches over medium-high heat for 2 minutes on each side. Place in a slightly overlapping row down the centre of the pan and spoon the sauce over the top, covering the chops completely. Cover the pan and cook over low heat for about 5 minutes. Sprinkle with parsley to serve.

Serves 4

Baked sea bass with wild rice stuffing

2 small fennel bulbs
65 g (⅓ cup) wild rice
250 ml (1 cup) fish stock
2 tablespoons butter
2 tablespoons olive oil
1 onion, chopped
1 garlic clove, crushed
grated zest of 1 lemon
2 kg (4 lb 8 oz) sea bass, bass or any
   large white fish, gutted and scaled
extra virgin olive oil
1 lemon, quartered
2 teaspoons chopped oregano
lemon wedges, to serve

Preheat the oven to 190°C (375°F/ Gas 5) and lightly grease a large, shallow ovenproof dish. Finely slice the fennel, reserving the green fronds.

Put the wild rice and stock in a saucepan with 3 tablespoons of water and bring to the boil. Simmer for 30 minutes, or until tender, then drain. Heat the butter and olive oil in a large frying pan and gently cook the fennel, onion and garlic for 12–15 minutes, or until softened but not browned. Add the lemon zest, stir in the rice and season with salt and pepper.

Put the fish on a chopping board. Stuff the fish with a heaped tablespoon of the fennel mixture and a quarter of the reserved fennel fronds. Transfer to an ovenproof dish. Brush with extra virgin olive oil, squeeze over the lemon and season well.

Spoon the remainder of the cooked fennel into the ovenproof dish and sprinkle with half the oregano. Put the fish on top of the fennel. Sprinkle the remaining oregano over the fish and loosely cover the dish with foil. Bake for 25 minutes, or until it is just cooked through. Serve with lemon wedges.

Serves 4

Braised sausages with puy lentils

1 tablespoon olive oil
110 g (4 oz) pancetta, cubed
2 red onions, finely chopped
12 Toulouse or pork sausages
2 garlic cloves, peeled and smashed
2 sprigs thyme leaves
300 g (1⅓ cup) Puy lentils
750 ml (3 cups) tinned chicken
  consommé
300 g (10½ oz) baby English spinach
  leaves, finely chopped
80 ml (⅓ cup) crème fraîche

Heat the oil in a wide heavy-based frying pan (one with a lid) and fry the pancetta until it is browned. Take it out using a slotted spoon, and put it in a bowl. Put the onion in the pan and cook until it is soft and only lightly browned. Take the onion out, using a slotted spoon, and add it to the pancetta. Put the sausages in the same pan and fry them until they are very brown all over. Put the pancetta and onion back in with the sausages.

Add the garlic and the thyme leaves to the frying pan, along with the lentils, and mix everything together. Add the consommé and bring to the boil. Put a lid on the frying pan and slowly simmer the mixture for 30–35 minutes, or until lentils are tender. Stir the spinach through.

Season the lentils with salt and pepper and·stir in the crème fraîche. Serve the sausages with the lentils in shallow bowls. Serve with bread.

Serves 4

Salmon nori roll with sesame noodles

300 g (10½ oz) soba noodles
1½ teaspoons sesame oil
2 tablespoons sesame seeds
2 pieces salmon fillet (10 x 15 cm/
  4 x 6 in), bones removed
2 sheets nori
1 tablespoon butter
250 g (9 oz) baby English spinach
  leaves

Cook the noodles in a large saucepan of boiling salted water for about 5 minutes, or until they are just cooked. The cooking time will vary depending on the brand of noodles. Drain the noodles, add the sesame oil and some seasoning, then toss them so they are coated in the oil. Dry-fry the sesame seeds in a frying pan until they start to colour and smell toasted, then add them to the noodles. Cover and keep warm.

Cut each salmon fillet in half horizontally and neaten the edges. Cut each sheet of nori in half with a pair of scissors and lay a piece of salmon fillet on top of each half. Season well, then roll up the fillets to make neat log shapes. Trim off any bits of nori or salmon that stick out. Using a sharp knife, cut each roll into three pieces.

Heat the butter in a non-stick frying pan and fry the pieces of roll until they are golden on each side and almost cooked all the way through. This will probably take about 4 minutes on each side. Lift out the rolls. Add the spinach to the pan, stir it around until it wilts, then turn off the heat. Serve the salmon with the noodles and some spinach on the side.

Serves 4

Lamb shanks with chickpeas

1 tablespoon oil
4 large or 8 small lamb shanks
2 onions, finely chopped
2 garlic cloves, crushed
1 tablespoon harissa
1 cinnamon stick
2 x 400 g (14 oz) cans chopped
    tomatoes
2 x 300 g (10½ oz) cans chickpeas,
    drained
90 g (3¼ oz) green olives
½ tablespoon preserved lemon or
    lemon zest, finely chopped
2 tablespoons mint, chopped

Heat the oil in a large casserole dish over a medium heat and fry the lamb shanks until they are well browned all over. Add the onion and garlic and fry them for a couple of minutes until the onion starts to soften.

Add the harissa, cinnamon and salt and pepper to the casserole, stir everything together, then add the chopped tomato and bring everything to the boil. If there doesn't seem to be enough liquid (the shanks need to be pretty well covered), add a bit of water. Put the lid on and turn the heat down until the liquid is simmering, then cook for 50 minutes.

Add the chickpeas, olives and lemon to the pan and stir them into the liquid. Season to taste and continue cooking with the lid off for another 20 to 30 minutes. By this time, the lamb should be very tender and almost falling off the bone. If it isn't, just keep cooking, checking every 5 minutes until it is. Using a big spoon, scoop any orange-coloured oil off the top, then stir in the mint. Serve with extra harissa if you would like the sauce a little hotter.

Serves 4

Grilled trout with lemon butter and couscous

200 g (1 cup) instant couscous
1 tablespoon olive oil
1 onion, finely chopped
4 pieces of red or yellow chargrilled
  capsicum (pepper), chopped
a small handful pine nuts
lemon juice and zest from 2 lemons
a large handful mint, chopped
4 rainbow trout fillets, with the skin
  removed
2 tablespoons butter, softened

Heat the grill (broiler). Bring 500 ml (2 cups) water to the boil in a saucepan and throw in the couscous. Take the pan off the heat and leave it to stand for 10 minutes.

Heat the oil in a frying pan and fry the onion until it is lightly browned. Add the capsicum and pine nuts, then stir in the couscous. Stir through half of the lemon juice and zest, along with the mint.

Put the trout fillets on an oiled baking tray. Mix the butter with the rest of the lemon zest and spread it on to the fish. Grill the fish for 6 minutes, or until it is just cooked through. Sprinkle on the rest of the lemon juice and season well.

Serve the trout (take it off the tray carefully as it hasn't got any skin to help hold it together) on the couscous with any buttery juices poured over it.

Serves 4

Lamb cutlets with onion marmalade

2 tablespoons butter
80 ml (⅓ cup) olive oil
4 onions, finely sliced
2 teaspoons brown sugar
2 teaspoons thyme leaves
2 tablespoons parsley, finely chopped
12 French-trimmed lamb cutlets
2 tablespoons lemon juice

Heat the butter and half the olive oil together in a saucepan. Add the onion, sugar and thyme and stir well. Turn the heat to low, cover the saucepan and cook the onion, stirring it occasionally for 30 to 35 minutes, or until it is very soft and golden. Season well, stir the parsley through and keep it warm over a very low heat.

Heat the remaining oil in a frying pan or brush a griddle with oil and, when it is hot, add the cutlets in a single layer. Fry for 2 minutes on each side, or until the lamb is browned on the outside but still feels springy when you press it. Add the lemon juice and season well.

Put a small pile of the onion and herb marmalade on each plate and place the cutlets around it.

Serves 4

Summer seafood marinara

300 g (10½ oz) fresh saffron angel
  hair pasta
1 tablespoon extra virgin olive oil
30 g (1 oz) butter
2 garlic cloves, finely chopped
1 large onion, finely chopped
1 small red chilli, finely chopped
600 g (1 lb 5 oz) can peeled
  tomatoes, chopped
250 ml (1 cup) white wine
zest of 1 lemon
½ tablespoon sugar
200 g (7 oz) scallops without roe
500 g (1 lb 2 oz) raw prawns (shrimp),
  peeled and deveined
300 g (10½ oz) clams (vongole)

Cook the pasta in a large saucepan
of rapidly boiling water until *al dente*.
Drain and keep warm.

Heat the oil and butter in a large frying
pan, add the garlic, onion and chilli
and cook over a medium heat for
5 minutes, or until soft but not golden.
Add the tomatoes and wine and bring
to the boil. Cook for 10 minutes, or
until the sauce has reduced and
thickened slightly.

Add the lemon zest, sugar, scallops,
prawns and clams and cook, covered,
for 5 minutes, or until the seafood is
tender. Discard any shells that do not
open. Season with salt and pepper.
Serve the sauce on top of the pasta.

Serves 4

Beef cooked in Guinness with celeriac purée

2 tablespoons oil
1 kg (2 lb 4 oz) chuck steak, cubed
2 onions, chopped
1 garlic clove, crushed
2 teaspoons brown sugar
2 teaspoons plain (all-purpose) flour
125 ml (½ cup) Guinness
375 ml (1½ cups) beef stock
1 bay leaf
2 sprigs thyme
1 celeriac
1 potato, cubed
250 ml (1 cup) milk
1 tablespoon butter
4 slices baguette, toasted
1 teaspoon Dijon mustard

Put the oven on to 180°C (350°F/ Gas 4). Heat half of the oil in a frying pan over a high heat and fry the meat in batches until it is browned all over. Add more oil as you need it. Put the meat in a casserole dish.

Add the onion to the frying pan and fry it gently over a low heat. When the onion starts to brown, add the garlic and brown sugar and cook until the onion is fairly brown. Stir in the flour, then transfer to the casserole dish.

Put the Guinness and stock in the frying pan and bring it to the boil, then pour into the casserole dish. Add the bay leaf and thyme to the casserole dish and season well. Bring to the boil, put a lid on and put the casserole in the oven for 2 hours.

Peel and chop the celeriac. Put the pieces into a bowl of water as you cut them. Put the potato and celeriac in a saucepan with the milk and bring to the boil. Cover and cook for 15 minutes, then mash everything together with the milk. Season well and add the butter.

Spread the bread with the mustard and serve with the beef ladled over and the celeriac purée on the side.

Serves 4

Roast lamb

2 rosemary sprigs
3 garlic cloves
75 g (2½ oz) pancetta
2 kg (4 lb 8 oz) leg of lamb, shank
   bone cut off just above the joint,
   trimmed of excess fat and tied
1 large onion
125 ml (½ cup) olive oil
375 ml (1½ cups) dry white wine

Preheat the oven to 230°C (450°F/ Gas 8). Strip the leaves off the rosemary sprigs and chop them with the garlic and pancetta until paste-like. Season with salt and pepper.

With the point of a sharp knife, make incisions about 1 cm (½ in) deep all over the lamb. Rub the rosemary filling over the surface of the lamb, pushing it into the incisions.

Cut the onion into four thick slices and put them in the centre of a roasting tin. Place the lamb on top and gently pour the olive oil over it. Roast for 15 minutes. Reduce the temperature to 180°C (350°F/Gas 4) and pour in 250 ml (1 cup) of the wine. Roast for 1½ hours for medium-rare, or longer if you prefer. Baste a couple of times and add a little water if the juices start to burn in the tin. Transfer the lamb to a carving platter and leave to rest for 10 minutes.

Remove the onion and spoon off the excess fat from the tin. Place over high heat on the stovetop, pour in the remaining wine and cook for 3–4 minutes, or until the sauce reduces and thickens. Taste for seasoning. Slice the lamb and serve with the sauce spooned over the top.

Pork chops with apples and cider

1 tablespoon oil
2 onions, sliced
2 Golden Delicious apples, cored and
  cut into wedges
2 teaspoons caster (superfine) sugar
2 teaspoons butter
4 thick pork chops, snipped around
  the edges
80 ml (⅓ cup) cider
80 ml (⅓ cup) cream

Heat the oil in a large non-stick frying pan, add the onion and fry for about 5 minutes, or until soft and just beginning to brown. Tip the onion out onto a plate.

Add the apple wedges to the pan and fry them for a minute or two — they should not break up, but should start to soften and brown. Add the sugar and butter and shake everything around in the pan until the apples start to caramelize. Transfer the apples to the plate with the onion.

Put the pork chops in the frying pan, add a bit of seasoning and fry them for 4 minutes on each side, or until they are cooked through. Put the onion and apple back in the pan and heat them up, then add the cider and bring to a simmer. Once the liquid is bubbling, add the cream and shake the pan so everything mixes together. Let it bubble for a minute, then season well and serve with potatoes and a green salad — watercress goes particularly well.

Serves 4

Thai mussels with noodles

2 kg (4 lb 8 oz) mussels
240 g (4 small bundles) glass noodles
2 garlic cloves, crushed
2 spring onions (scallions), finely
  chopped
2 tablespoons red curry paste
160 ml ($\frac{2}{3}$ cup) coconut cream
juice of 2 limes
2 tablespoons fish sauce
a handful coriander (cilantro) leaves

Rinse the mussels in cold water and pull off any beards. Now look at each one individually and, if it isn't tightly closed, tap it on the work surface to see if it will close. Throw away any mussels that won't close.

Soak the noodles in boiling water for a minute or two. Drain them and, using a pair of scissors, cut them into shorter lengths.

Put the mussels in a deep frying pan or wok with the garlic and spring onion and 125 ml ($\frac{1}{2}$ cup) water. Bring the water to the boil, then put a lid on and cook the mussels for 2 to 3 minutes, shaking occasionally, or until they are all open. Throw away any that don't open. Tip the whole lot, including any liquid, into a sieve lined with a piece of muslin, reserving the liquid.

Pour the cooking liquid back into the pan, add the curry paste and coconut cream and stir together. Bring the mixture to the boil, then add the lime juice and fish sauce. Put the mussels back in the pan. Cook for a minute, then stir in the coriander leaves.

Put some noodles in each bowl and ladle the mussels on top.

Serves 4

Saltimbocca

8 small veal escalopes
8 slices prosciutto
8 sage leaves
2 tablespoons olive oil
60 g (2¼ oz) butter
185 ml (¾ cup) dry Marsala or
  dry white wine

Place the veal between two sheets of greaseproof paper and pound with a meat mallet or rolling pin until they are 5 mm (¼ in) thick. Make sure you pound them evenly. Peel off the paper and season lightly. Cut the prosciutto slices to the same size as the veal. Cover each piece of veal with a slice of prosciutto and place a sage leaf in the centre. Secure the sage leaf with a cocktail stick.

Heat the olive oil and half the butter in a large frying pan. Add the veal in batches and fry, prosciutto side up, over medium heat for 3–4 minutes, or until the veal is just cooked through. Briefly flip the saltimbocca over and fry the prosciutto side. Transfer each batch to a warm plate as it is done.

Pour off the oil from the pan and add the Marsala or wine. Bring to the boil and cook over high heat until reduced by half, scraping up the bits from the bottom of the pan. Add the remaining butter and, when it has melted, season the sauce. Remove the cocktail sticks and spoon the sauce over the veal to serve.

Serves 4

Steak with maître d'hotel butter

90 g (3¼ oz) unsalted butter, softened
2 teaspoons finely chopped parsley
lemon juice
4 steaks, about 1.5 cm (⁵/₈ in) thick
1 tablespoon olive oil

Beat the butter to a cream in a bowl, using a wooden spoon, then beat in a pinch of salt, a pinch of pepper and the parsley. Next add about 2 teaspoons of lemon juice, a few drops at a time. Let the butter harden in the fridge a little, then form it into a log shape by rolling it up in greaseproof paper. Put it into the fridge until you need it.

Season the steaks with salt and pepper on both sides. Heat the oil in a large frying pan and, when it is very hot, add the steaks. Cook them for 2 minutes on each side for rare, 3 minutes on each side for medium, and 4 minutes on each side for well done. The timings may vary depending on the thickness of your steaks — if they are thin, give them a slightly shorter time and if they are thick, cook them for longer.

Cut the butter into slices and put a couple of slices on top of each steak. The heat of the steak will melt the butter. Serve with potatoes and vegetables or salad.

Serves 4

Silverside with parsley sauce

1.5 kg (3 lb 5 oz) corned silverside
1 teaspoon black peppercorns
5 cloves
2 bay leaves, torn
2 tablespoons soft brown sugar

Parsley sauce
50 g (1³/₄ oz) butter
1¹/₂ tablespoons plain (all-purpose)
   flour
400 ml (14 fl oz) milk
125 ml (¹/₂ cup) beef stock
2 tablespoons chopped parsley

Soak the corned beef in cold water for 45 minutes, changing the water 3–4 times. This helps eliminate some of the salty flavour.

Lift the beef out of the water and put it in a large heavy-based saucepan with the peppercorns, cloves, bay leaves, brown sugar and enough cold water to just cover it. Bring to the boil, then reduce the heat to very low and simmer for 1¹/₂–1³/₄ hours. Turn the meat over every half hour and keep an eye on the water level — you'll probably need to add some more. You don't want the water to boil or the meat will become tough, so use a heat diffuser mat if you need to. Remove the meat from the pan and let it rest for 15 minutes.

To make the parsley sauce, melt the butter in a saucepan over medium heat and then stir in the flour and keep stirring for 1 minute. Take the pan off the heat and pour in the milk and stock, whisking until smooth. Return the pan to the heat and cook, whisking constantly, until the sauce boils and thickens. Reduce the heat and simmer for 2 minutes more before stirring in the parsley and a little salt and pepper. Serve over slices of silverside with steamed vegetables.

Serves 6

Sweets

Double chocolate brownies

80 g (2³/₄ oz) butter
40 g (¹/₃ cup) cocoa powder
145 g (²/₃ cup) caster (superfine)
  sugar
2 eggs
60 g (¹/₂ cup) plain (all-purpose) flour
¹/₂ teaspoon baking powder
100 g (¹/₂ cup) chocolate chips

Preheat the oven on to 180°C (350°F/
Gas 4). Brush your cake tin with oil or
melted butter, put a piece of baking
paper in the bottom.

Melt the butter in a saucepan. When
it is ready, take it off the heat and stir
in the cocoa and sugar, followed by
the eggs.

Put a sieve over the saucepan and tip
in the flour and baking powder, along
with a pinch of salt. Sift everything
into the saucepan, then mix it in.
Make sure you don't have any
pockets of flour. Add the chocolate
chips and stir them in.

Pour the mixture into your tin and
bake it for 30 minutes. If you have
used a different sized tin, the cooking
time may be shorter (bigger tin) or
longer (smaller tin). You will know your
brownies are cooked when you can
poke a skewer or knife into the middle
of them and it comes out clean.
Remember though, the chocolate
chips may have melted and if your
skewer hits one of those, it might look
as if the mixture is still wet. Leave the
slab to cool in the tin, then tip it out
and cut it into brownie pieces.

Makes 12

Tropical meringues

3 egg whites
175 g (³/₄ cup) caster (superfine)
  sugar
50 g (¹/₂ cup) desiccated coconut
¹/₄ teaspoon coconut essence
2 tablespoons milk
2 tablespoons caster (superfine) sugar
250 g (9 oz) mascarpone cheese
2 mangoes, peeled and thinly sliced
2 passionfruit

Preheat the oven to 140°C (275°F/ Gas 1). Grease and line two baking trays with baking paper. Put the egg whites in a bowl and whisk until soft peaks form. Add the sugar, 1 tablespoon at a time, until the mixture is glossy. Fold in the desiccated coconut and coconut essence.

Spoon 8 cm (3 in) mounds of the mixture onto the trays. Bake for 1 hour. Turn the oven off and leave for a further hour.

Add the milk and sugar to the mascarpone and whisk well. Dollop a little onto each meringue and top with the fruit.

Makes 6

Choc-chip and pistachio friands

150 g (5½ oz) shelled pistachio nuts
60 g (½ cup) plain (all-purpose) flour
175 g (6 oz) unsalted butter
210 g (1⅔ cups) icing (confectioners')
  sugar
2 tablespoons cocoa
½ teaspoon ground cardamom
5 egg whites, lightly whisked
200 g (7 oz) chocolate chips
icing (confectioners') sugar, to dust

Preheat the oven to 200°C (400°F/ Gas 6). Grease and line ten friand tins, or ten 125 ml (½ cup) capacity muffin holes. Place the pistachios on a baking tray and roast for 5 minutes. Remove from the oven and allow to cool. Place the pistachios and flour in a food processor and process until finely ground.

Place the butter and icing sugar in a bowl and beat until light and creamy. Sift together the pistachios and flour with the cocoa and cardamom, and fold into the creamed mixture.

Stir the egg whites into the creamed mixture, together with the chocolate chips, and mix to combine. Spoon the mixture into the prepared tins and bake for 25–30 minutes, or until they come away from the sides of the tin. Cool on wire racks. Dust lightly with icing sugar.

Makes 10

Choc-hazelnut puff pastry rolls

80 g (2³/₄ oz) choc-hazelnut spread
80 g (²/₃ cup) icing (confectioners')
  sugar
2 sheets puff pastry, thawed
1 egg, lightly beaten
icing (confectioners') sugar, to dust

Preheat the oven to 200°C (400°F/ Gas 6). Combine the choc-hazelnut spread and icing sugar and roll into a 20 cm (8 in) long roll. Wrap the roll in plastic wrap and twist the ends to enclose. Refrigerate for 30 minutes. When firm, cut the roll into eight even pieces. Roll each of the pieces in icing sugar.

Cut each sheet of puff pastry into four squares. Place a piece of the choc-hazelnut mixture roll onto each square of pastry and roll up to enclose. Pinch the ends and brush lightly with egg. Bake for 15 minutes, or until the pastry is golden.

Dust with icing sugar.

Serves 4

High-top cappuccino and white-choc muffins

20 g (¼ cup) instant espresso coffee
  powder
1 tablespoon boiling water
310 g (2½ cups) self-raising flour
115 g (½ cup) caster (superfine) sugar
2 eggs, lightly beaten
375 ml (1½ cups) buttermilk
1 teaspoon vanilla essence
150 g (5½ oz) butter, melted
100 g (3½ oz) white chocolate,
  roughly chopped
30 g (1 oz) butter, extra
3 tablespoons brown sugar

Preheat the oven to 200°C (400°F/ Gas 6). Cut eight lengths of baking paper and roll into 8 cm (3 in) high cylinders to fit into eight 125 ml (½-cup) capacity ramekins. When in place in the ramekins, secure the cylinders with string and place all the ramekins onto a baking tray.

Dissolve the coffee in the boiling water and allow to cool. Sift the flour and sugar into a bowl. Combine the egg, buttermilk, vanilla, melted butter, white chocolate and the coffee mixture and roughly combine with the dry ingredients. Spoon the mixture into each cylinder.

Heat the extra butter and the brown sugar and stir until the sugar dissolves. Spoon this mixture onto each muffin and gently swirl into the muffin using a skewer. Bake for 25–30 minutes, or until risen and cooked when tested with a skewer.

Makes 8

Nursery rice pudding

140 g (²/₃ cup) arborio or short-grain
  rice
1 litre (4 cups) milk
80 g (¹/₃ cup) caster (superfine) sugar
1 teaspoon vanilla extract
125 ml (¹/₂ cup) cream

Rinse the rice in a colander until the
water runs clear. Drain well and place
in a heavy-based pan with the milk,
sugar and vanilla.

Bring to the boil while stirring, then
reduce the heat to the lowest setting
and cook for about 45 minutes,
stirring frequently, until the rice is thick
and creamy.

Remove the pan from the heat and
leave to stand for 10 minutes. Stir in
the cream. Serve warm with stewed
fruit, if desired.

Serves 4–6

Variations: Add a cinnamon stick and
a strip of lemon zest to the rice in
place of vanilla extract. Or add a small
sprig of washed lavender to the rice
while cooking.

Zabaglione

6 egg yolks
3 tablespoons caster (superfine) sugar
125 ml (1/2 cup) sweet Marsala
250 ml (1 cup) thick (double/heavy)
   cream

Whisk the egg yolks and sugar in the top of a double boiler or in a heatproof bowl set over a saucepan of simmering water. Make sure that the base of the bowl does not touch the water or the egg may overcook and stick. It is important that you whisk constantly to move the cooked mixture from the outside of the bowl to the centre.

When the mixture is tepid, add the Marsala and whisk for another 5 minutes, or until it has thickened enough to hold its shape when drizzled off the whisk into the bowl.

Whip the cream until soft peaks form. Gently fold in the egg yolk and Marsala mixture. Divide among four glasses or bowls. Cover and refrigerate for 3–4 hours before serving.

Serves 4

Grandmother's pavlova

4 egg whites
230 g (1 cup) caster (superfine) sugar
2 teaspoons cornflour (cornstarch)
1 teaspoon white vinegar
500 ml (2 cups) cream
3 passionfruit, to decorate
strawberries, to decorate

Preheat the oven to warm 160°C (315°F/Gas 2–3). Line a 32 x 28 cm (13 x 11 in) baking tray with baking paper.

Place the egg whites and a pinch of salt in a small, dry bowl. Using electric beaters, beat until stiff peaks form. Add the sugar gradually, beating constantly after each addition, until the mixture is thick and glossy and all the sugar has dissolved.

Using a metal spoon, fold in the cornflour and vinegar. Spoon the mixture into a mound on the prepared tray. Lightly flatten the top of the pavlova and smooth the sides. (This pavlova should have a cake shape and be about 2.5 cm (1 in) high.) Bake for 1 hour, or until pale cream and crisp. Remove from the oven while warm and carefully turn upside down onto a plate. Allow to cool.

Lightly whip the cream until soft peaks form and spread over the soft centre. Decorate with pulp from the passionfruit and halved strawberries. Cut into wedges to serve.

Serves 6

Trifle

4 slices of Madeira (pound) cake or
  trifle sponges
3 tablespoons sweet sherry or
  Madeira
250 g (9 oz) raspberries
4 eggs
2 tablespoons caster (superfine) sugar
2 tablespoons plain (all-purpose) flour
500 ml (2 cups) milk
1/4 teaspoon vanilla extract
125 ml (1/2 cup) cream, whipped
3 tablespoons flaked almonds, to
  decorate
raspberries, to decorate

Put the cake in the base of a bowl,
then sprinkle it with the sherry. Scatter
the raspberries over the top and
crush them gently into the sponge
with the back of a spoon to release
their tart flavour, leaving some of
them whole.

Mix the eggs, sugar and flour together
in a bowl. Heat the milk in a pan, pour
it over the egg mixture, stir well and
pour back into a clean pan. Cook
over medium heat until the custard
boils and thickens and coats the back
of a spoon. Stir in the vanilla, cover
the surface with plastic wrap and
leave to cool.

Pour the cooled custard over the
raspberries and leave to set in
the fridge — it will firm up but not
become solid. Spoon the whipped
cream over the custard. Go wild
decorating with almonds and
raspberries (or anything else you
fancy) and refrigerate until needed.

Serves 6

Creamy chocolate mousse

125 g (4½ oz) good-quality dark
  chocolate, chopped
4 eggs, separated
185 ml (¾ cup) cream, lightly
  whipped
cocoa powder, to serve

Melt the chocolate in a bowl balanced over a saucepan of gently simmering water (make sure the base of the bowl does not touch the water). Stir the chocolate occasionally until it's melted, then take it off the heat to cool slightly. Lightly beat the egg yolks and stir them into the melted chocolate, then gently fold in the cream until velvety.

Beat the egg whites to soft peaks. Fold one spoonful of the fluffy egg white into the mousse with a metal spoon, then gently fold in the remainder — the secret is to use a light, quick touch.

You only need small quantities of the mousse — you can either serve it in six small wine glasses or 185 ml (¾ cup) ramekins. Cover with plastic wrap and refrigerate for 4 hours, or overnight until set. When you're ready to serve, add a curl of whipped cream and a dusting of cocoa powder.

Serves 6

Banana fritters

125 g (1 cup) self-raising flour
1 tablespoon caster (superfine) sugar
1 teaspoon ground cinnamon
4 bananas
oil, for deep-frying
ice cream, to serve

Sift the flour and a pinch of salt into a bowl. Make a well in the centre, and gradually add 250 ml (1 cup) water while gently whisking, drawing the flour in from the sides. Whisk until just combined. Don't worry if the batter looks a bit lumpy. Stand for 30 minutes. Combine the sugar and cinnamon in a bowl, and set aside.

Cut the bananas in half crossways, slightly on the diagonal. Dip them into the batter. Quickly drain off any excess batter and deep-fry for 2 minutes, or until crisp and golden. The best way to do this is to use two pairs of tongs — one to dip the bananas in the batter and lift into the oil, and one to remove from the oil. You could also use a slotted spoon to lift the cooked fritters. Drain on paper towels. Repeat with the remaining bananas. Sprinkle with the cinnamon sugar and serve with ice cream.

Serves 4

Baked cheesecake

375 g (13 oz) plain sweet biscuits
175 g (6 oz) unsalted butter, melted

Filling
500 g (1 lb 2 oz) cream cheese
200 g (7 oz) caster (superfine) sugar
4 eggs
300 ml (10½ fl oz) whipping cream
2 tablespoons plain (all-purpose) flour
1 teaspoon ground cinnamon
¼ teaspoon freshly grated nutmeg
1 tablespoons lemon juice
2 teaspoon vanilla extract
freshly grated nutmeg
ground cinnamon

Process the biscuits in a food processor until they are crushed into fine crumbs. Add the melted butter and process for another 10 seconds. Press the mixture into the base and side of a lightly greased 23 cm (9 in) shallow springform tin, then place it in the fridge for an hour.

Beat the cream cheese and sugar together, then add the eggs and cream and beat for about 4 minutes. Fold in the flour, cinnamon, nutmeg, lemon juice and vanilla. Pour the mixture into the chilled crust. Bake in a 180°C (350°F/Gas 4) oven for an hour without opening the oven door, until the cheesecake is golden brown on top.

Turn off the heat and let the cake stand in the oven for 2 hours. Then open the oven door and let it stand for a further hour. Lastly, refrigerate overnight.

For a decorative touch, sprinkle with nutmeg and cinnamon and then serve. Delicious with lashings of cream and some strawberries.

Serves 10

Chocolate croissant pudding

4 croissants, torn into pieces
125 g (4½ oz) good-quality dark
 chocolate, chopped into pieces
4 eggs
5 tablespoons caster (superfine) sugar
250 ml (1 cup) milk
250 ml (1 cup) cream
3 teaspoons orange liqueur
3 teaspoons grated orange zest
4 tablespoons orange juice
2 tablespoons roughly chopped
 hazelnuts
cream, to serve

Preheat the oven to 180°C (350°F/ Gas 4). Grease the base and side of a 20 cm (8 in) deep-sided cake tin and line the bottom of the tin with baking paper. Put the croissant pieces into the tin, then scatter over 100 g (3½ oz) chocolate pieces.

Beat the eggs and sugar together until pale and creamy. Heat the milk, cream and liqueur and remaining chocolate pieces in a saucepan until almost boiling. Stir to melt the chocolate, then remove the pan from the heat. Gradually add to the egg mixture, stirring constantly. Next, stir in the orange zest and juice. Slowly pour the mixture over the croissants, allowing the liquid to be fully absorbed before adding more.

Sprinkle the hazelnuts over the top and bake for 50 minutes, or until a skewer comes out clean when inserted into the centre. Cool for 10 minutes. Turn the pudding out and invert onto a serving plate. Slice and serve warm with a dollop of cream.

Serves 6–8

Baked rice pudding

55 g (¼ cup) pudding, short- or
  medium-grain rice
410 ml (1²/₃ cups) milk
1½ tablespoons caster (superfine)
  sugar
185 ml (¾ cup) cream
¼ teaspoon vanilla extract
¼ teaspoon grated nutmeg
1 bay leaf (optional)

Preheat the oven to 150°C (300°F/
Gas 2) and grease four 250 ml (1 cup)
ramekins. In a bowl, mix together the
rice, milk, caster sugar, cream and
vanilla extract, and pour into the
greased dish. Dust the surface with
the grated nutmeg and float the bay
leaf on top for a little extra flavour.

Bake the rice puddings for about
1 hour, until the rice has absorbed
most of the milk, the texture is creamy
and a brown skin has formed on top.
Serve hot.

Serves 4

Eton mess

4–6 ready-made meringues
250 g (9 oz) strawberries
1 teaspoon caster (superfine) sugar
250 ml (1 cup) thick (double/heavy)
   cream

Break the meringues into pieces. Cut the strawberries into quarters and put them in a bowl with the sugar. Using a potato masher or the back of a spoon, squash them slightly so they start to become juicy. Whip the cream with a balloon or electric whisk until it is quite thick but not solid.

Mix everything together gently and spoon it into glasses.

Serves 4

Lemon pudding with citrus cream

60 g (2¼ oz) butter, softened
185 g (¾ cup) sugar
2 teaspoons grated lemon zest
3 eggs, separated
30 g (¼ cup) self-raising flour
185 ml (¾ cup) milk
80 ml (⅓ cup) lemon juice

Citrus cream
300 ml (10½ fl oz) thick
   (double/heavy) cream
2 tablespoons icing (confectioners')
   sugar
grated zest of 1 orange
grated zest of ½ lime

Preheat the oven to 180°C (350°F/ Gas 4). Lightly grease a 1 litre (4 cup) round ovenproof or soufflé dish. Put the butter, sugar and lemon zest in a bowl and beat until light and well combined.

Add the egg yolks gradually, beating well after each addition. Add the flour and milk alternately to make a smooth but not runny batter. Stir in the lemon juice. The batter may look to have separated at this stage, but this is fine.

In a separate bowl, whisk the egg whites until firm (but not dry) peaks form, then use a metal spoon to gently fold the whites into the batter. Pour the batter into the ovenproof dish and place into a roasting tin. Fill the tin with enough boiling water to come one-third of the way up the outside of the dish. Cook for 40–45 minutes, or until risen and firm to the touch. Allow to stand for 10 minutes before serving.

Meanwhile, make the citrus cream. Whip the cream with the sugar until soft peaks form. Fold in the grated orange and lime zest. Dust the pudding with icing sugar, if you like, and serve with the citrus cream.

Serves 4–6

Individual sticky date cakes

270 g (1 1/2 cups) pitted dates, chopped
1 teaspoon bicarbonate of soda
150 g (5 1/2 oz) unsalted butter, chopped
185 g (1 1/2 cups) self-raising flour
265 g (9 1/2 oz) brown sugar
2 eggs, lightly beaten
2 tablespoons golden syrup (dark corn syrup)
185 ml (3/4 cup) cream

Preheat the oven to 180°C (350°F/ Gas 4). Grease six 250 ml (1 cup) muffin tin holes. Put the dates and 250 ml (1 cup) water in a saucepan, bring to the boil, then remove from the heat and stir in the bicarbonate of soda. Add 60 g (1/4 cup) of the butter and stir until melted.

Sift the flour into a large bowl, then stir in 125 g (1/2 cup) of the sugar. Make a well in the centre, add the date mixture and egg and stir until combined. Evenly divide the mixture among the muffin holes and bake for 20 minutes, or until a skewer comes out clean when inserted into the centre.

To make the sauce, put the golden syrup, cream, the remaining butter and sugar in a small saucepan and stir over low heat for about 4 minutes, or until the sugar has dissolved. Bring to the boil, then reduce the heat and simmer, stirring occasionally, for 2 minutes.

To serve, put the warm cakes onto serving plates, pierce a few times with a skewer and drizzle over the sauce. Serve with ice cream, if desired.

Makes 6

Spiced fruit salad

110 g (½ cup) caster (superfine) sugar
4 slices ginger
1 bird's eye chilli, cut in half
juice and zest of 2 limes
fruit, a mixture of watermelon, melon,
  mango, banana, cherries, lychees,
  kiwi fruit, or anything else you fancy
  — enough for 4 portions

Put the sugar in a saucepan with 125 ml (½ cup) water and the ginger and chilli. Heat it until the sugar melts, then leave it to cool before adding the lime juice and zest. Take out the ginger and chilli.

Put your selection of fruit into a bowl and pour the syrup over it. Leave it to marinate in the fridge for 30 minutes. Serve with coconut ice cream or any other kind of ice cream or sorbet.

Serves 4

Crème caramel

Caramel
100 g (3½ oz) caster (superfine) sugar

650 ml (22 fl oz) milk
1 vanilla pod
125 g (4½ oz) caster (superfine) sugar
3 eggs, beaten
3 egg yolks

To make the caramel, put the sugar in a heavy-based saucepan and heat until it dissolves and starts to caramelize — tip the saucepan from side to side as the sugar cooks to keep the colouring even. Remove from the heat and carefully add 2 tablespoons water to stop the cooking process. Pour into six 125 ml (½ cup) ramekins and leave to cool.

Preheat the oven to 180°C (350°F/ Gas 4). Put the milk and vanilla pod in a saucepan and bring just to the boil. Mix together the sugar, egg and egg yolks. Strain the boiling milk over the egg mixture and stir well. Ladle into the ramekins and place in a roasting tin. Pour enough hot water into the tin to come halfway up the sides of the ramekins. Cook for 35–40 minutes, or until firm to the touch. Remove from the tin and leave for 15 minutes. Unmould onto plates and pour on any leftover caramel.

Serves 6

Zuppa inglese

4 thick slices sponge or Madeira cake
80 ml (1/3 cup) kirsch
150 g (5 1/2 oz) raspberries
170 g (6 oz) blackberries
2 tablespoons caster (superfine) sugar
250 ml (1 cup) custard
250 ml (1 cup) cream, lightly whipped
icing (confectioners') sugar, to dust

Put a piece of sponge cake on each of four deep plates and brush or sprinkle it with the kirsch. Leave the kirsch to soak in for at least a minute or two.

Put the raspberries and blackberries in a saucepan with the caster sugar. Gently warm through over a low heat so that the sugar just melts, then leave the fruit to cool.

Spoon the fruit over the sponge, pour the custard on top of the fruit and, finally, dollop the cream on top and dust with icing sugar.

Serves 4

Baked apples

6 cooking apples
75 g (2¹/₂ oz) unsalted butter, chilled
6 small cinnamon sticks
100 g (3¹/₂ oz) pistachio nuts or pine
  nuts
3 tablespoons brown sugar
100 g (3¹/₂ oz) raisins or sultanas
200 ml (7 fl oz) grappa

Preheat the oven to 175°C (350°F/ Gas 3). Remove the cores from the apples with a sharp knife or corer and place the apples in an ovenproof dish.

Divide the butter into six sticks and push it into the core of the apples. Push a cinnamon stick into the middle of each apple and scatter with the nuts, sugar and raisins. Finally, pour over the grappa.

Bake for 30–35 minutes, basting the apples occasionally with the juices in the dish until they are soft when tested with a skewer.

Serves 4

Mango fool

2 very ripe mangoes
250 ml (1 cup) Greek-style yoghurt
80 ml (⅓ cup) cream

Take the flesh off the mangoes. The easiest way to do this is to slice down either side of the stone so you have two 'cheeks'. Make crisscross cuts through the mango flesh on each cheek, almost through to the skin, then turn each cheek inside out and slice the flesh from the skin into a bowl. Cut the rest of the flesh from the stone.

Purée the flesh either by using a food processor or blender, or if you don't have any of these, just mash the flesh thoroughly.

Put a spoonful of mango purée in the bottom of four small glasses, bowls or cups, put a spoonful of yoghurt on top and then repeat. Spoon half the cream over each serving when you have used up all the mango and yoghurt. Swirl the layers together just before you eat them.

Serves 4

Tiramisu

5 eggs, separated
180 g (6 oz) caster (superfine) sugar
250 g (9 oz) mascarpone cheese
250 ml (1 cup) cold very strong coffee
3 tablespoons brandy or sweet
  Marsala
44 small sponge fingers
80 g (2¾ oz) dark chocolate, finely
  grated

Beat the egg yolks with the sugar until the sugar has dissolved and the mixture is light and fluffy and leaves a ribbon trail when dropped from the whisk. Add the mascarpone and beat until the mixture is smooth. Whisk the egg whites in a clean dry glass bowl until soft peaks form. Fold into the mascarpone mixture.

Pour the coffee into a shallow dish and add the brandy. Dip some of the sponge finger biscuits into the coffee mixture, using enough biscuits to cover the base of a 25 cm (10 in) square dish. The biscuits should be fairly well soaked on both sides but not so much so that they break up. Arrange the biscuits in one tightly packed layer in the base of the dish.

Spread half the mascarpone mixture over the layer of biscuits. Add another layer of soaked biscuits and then another layer of mascarpone, smoothing the top layer neatly. Leave to rest in the fridge for at least 2 hours or overnight. Dust with the grated chocolate to serve.

Serves 4

White chocolate creams

250 ml (1 cup) thick (double/heavy)
  cream
4 cardamom pods, slightly crushed
1 bay leaf
150 g (5½ oz) white chocolate
3 egg yolks

Put the cream, cardamom and bay leaf in a saucepan and gently bring the mixture to the boil. Remove from the heat and set aside so the cardamom and bay leaf flavours infuse into the cream.

Grate or finely chop the white chocolate — this will make it melt much faster and also lessen the chance of it all going lumpy — and put it in a bowl. Gently heat the cream up again until it is almost boiling and then pour it through a sieve (to strain out the cardamom and bay leaf) over the chocolate. Stir until the chocolate has dissolved. Gently whisk the egg yolks and stir them into the mixture.

Pour the mixture into four espresso cups or really small bowls and put them in the fridge to set. They should be ready in a couple of hours.

Serves 4

Panna cotta

450 ml (16 fl oz) thick (double/heavy) cream
4 tablespoons caster (superfine) sugar
2 tablespoons grappa (optional)
vanilla extract
3 leaves or 1 ¼ teaspoons gelatine
250 g (9 oz) berries, to serve

Put the cream and sugar in a saucepan and stir over gentle heat until the sugar has dissolved. Bring to the boil, then simmer for 3 minutes, adding the grappa and a few drops of vanilla extract to taste.

If you are using the gelatine leaves, soak them in cold water until floppy, then squeeze out any excess water. Stir the leaves into the hot cream until they are completely dissolved. If you are using powdered gelatine, sprinkle it onto the hot cream in an even layer and leave it to sponge for a minute, then stir it into the cream until dissolved.

Pour the mixture into four 125 ml (½ cup) metal or ceramic ramekins, cover each with a piece of plastic wrap and refrigerate until set.

Unmould the panna cotta by placing the ramekins very briefly in a bowl of hot water and then tipping them gently onto plates. Metal ramekins will take a shorter time than ceramic to unmould as they heat up quickly. Serve with the fresh berries.

Serves 4

Fig and raspberry cake

185 g (6¹/₄ oz) unsalted butter
185 g (6¹/₄ oz) caster (superfine)
  sugar, plus extra for sprinkling
1 egg, plus 1 egg yolk
335 g (2²/₃ cups) plain (all-purpose)
  flour
1 teaspoon baking powder
4 figs, quartered
grated zest of 1 orange
200 g (7 oz) raspberries

Preheat the oven to 180°C (350°F/ Gas 4). Lightly grease a 23 cm (9 in) springform tin. Cream the butter and sugar until light. Add the egg and yolk and beat again. Sift in the flour, baking powder and pinch of salt, and combine to form a dough. Chill until firm.

Divide the dough in two and roll one piece out large enough to cover the base of the tin. Transfer it to the prepared tin and set in place, pressing the dough up the sides a little. Cover with the figs, orange zest and raspberries. Roll out the remaining dough and place it over the filling. Brush with water and sprinkle with a little sugar. Bake for 30 minutes and serve warm.

Serves 6

Chocolate pudding

160 g (6 oz) dark chocolate, chopped
butter, for greasing
80 g (2³/₄ oz) caster (superfine) sugar
60 g (2¹/₄ oz) milk chocolate, chopped
4 eggs
cream, to serve

Put the oven on to 200°C (400°F/
Gas 6). Put the dark chocolate in a
glass bowl and set it above a pan of
simmering water. The chocolate will
gradually start to soften and look
glossy — when it does this, stir it until
it is smooth.

Grease the inside of four 200 ml
(7 fl oz) ramekins with butter. Add
¹/₂ teaspoon of the sugar to each and
shake it around until the insides are
coated. Divide the chopped milk
chocolate among the ramekins.

Beat the rest of the sugar with the
egg yolks, using electric beaters, for
about 3 minutes, or until you have a
pale, creamy mass. Clean the beaters
and dry them thoroughly. Whisk the
egg whites until they are thick enough
to stand up in peaks.

Fold the melted chocolate into the
yolk mixture and then fold in the
whites. Use a large spoon or rubber
spatula to do this and try not to
squash out too much air. Divide the
mixture among the four ramekins.
Bake for 15–20 minutes. The
puddings should be puffed and
spongelike. Serve straight away
with cream.

Serves 4

Sticky black rice pudding with mangoes

400 g (2 cups) black sticky rice
3 fresh pandanus leaves
500 ml (2 cups) coconut milk
85 g (3 oz) palm sugar, grated
3 tablespoons caster (superfine) sugar
coconut cream, to serve
mango or papaya cubes, to serve

Put the rice in a large glass or ceramic bowl and cover with water. Leave to soak for at least 8 hours, or overnight. Drain, then put in a saucepan with 1 litre (4 cups) of water and slowly bring to the boil. Cook at a slow boil, stirring frequently, for 20 minutes, or until tender. Drain.

Shred the pandanus leaves with your fingers, then tie them in a knot. Pour the coconut milk into a large saucepan and heat until almost boiling. Add the palm sugar, caster sugar and pandanus leaves, and stir until the sugar is dissolved.

Add the rice to the pan and cook, stirring, for about 8 minutes without boiling. Remove from the heat, cover and leave for 15 minutes to absorb the flavours. Remove the pandanus leaves.

Spoon the rice into individual bowls and serve warm with coconut cream and fresh mango or papaya cubes.

Serves 6

Coffee gelato

5 egg yolks
115 g (½ cup) sugar
500 ml (2 cups) milk
125 ml (½ cup) freshly made
  espresso
1 tablespoon Tia Maria or coffee
  liqueur

Whisk the egg yolks and half the sugar in a bowl until you have a pale and creamy mixture. Pour the milk and coffee into a saucepan, add the remaining sugar and bring to the boil. Add to the egg mixture and whisk together. Pour back into the saucepan and cook over low heat, taking care that the custard doesn't boil. Stir constantly until the mixture is thick enough to coat the back of a wooden spoon. Strain the custard into a bowl and cool over ice before adding the Tia Maria.

To make the gelato by hand, pour the mixture into a freezerproof container, cover and freeze. Break up the ice crystals every 30 minutes with a fork to ensure a smooth texture. Repeat until it is ready — this may take 4 hours. If using an ice cream machine, follow the manufacturer's instructions.

Serves 6

Apple crumble

8 apples
90 g (⅓ cup) caster (superfine) sugar
zest of 1 lemon
120 g (4 oz) butter
125 g (1 cup) plain (all-purpose) flour
1 teaspoon ground cinnamon
cream, to serve

Turn the oven to 180°C (350°/Gas 4). Peel and core the apples, then cut them into chunks. Put the apple, 2 tablespoons of the sugar and the lemon zest in a small baking dish and mix them together. Dot 2 tablespoons of butter over the top.

Rub the remaining butter into the flour until you have a texture that resembles coarse breadcrumbs. Stir in the rest of the sugar and the cinnamon. Add 1–2 tablespoons of water and stir the crumbs together so they form bigger clumps.

Sprinkle the crumble mixture over the apple and bake the crumble for 1 hour 15 minutes, by which time the top should be browned and the juice bubbling up through the crumble. Serve with cream.

Serves 4

Fruit poached in red wine

3 pears, peeled, quartered and cored
3 apples, peeled, quartered and
   cored
50 g (1³/₄ oz) sugar
1 vanilla pod, cut in half lengthways
2 small cinnamon sticks
400 ml (14 fl oz) red wine
200 ml (7 fl oz) dessert wine or port
700 g (1 lb 9 oz) red-skinned plums,
   halved

Put the pears and apples in a large saucepan. Add the sugar, vanilla pod, cinnamon sticks, red wine and dessert wine and bring to the boil. Reduce the heat and gently simmer for about 5–10 minutes, or until just soft.

Add the plums, stirring them through the pears and apples, and bring the liquid back to a simmer. Cook for another 5 minutes, or until the plums are soft.

Remove the saucepan from the heat, cover with a lid and leave the fruit to marinate in the syrup for at least 6 hours. Reheat gently to serve warm or serve at room temperature with cream or ice cream and a biscuit.

Serves 6

Coffee granita

200 g (7 oz) caster (superfine) sugar
1.25 litres (5 cups) very strong
  espresso coffee
ice cream, to serve

Heat the caster sugar with 25 ml
(½ fl oz) hot water in a saucepan until
the sugar dissolves. Simmer for
3 minutes to make a sugar syrup.
Add the coffee and stir well.

Pour into a plastic or metal freezer
box. The mixture should be no deeper
than 3 cm (1¼ in) so that the granita
freezes quickly and breaks up easily.
Stir every 2 hours with a fork to break
up the ice crystals as they form.
Repeat this two or three times. The
granita is ready when almost set but
still grainy. Stir a fork through it just
before serving. Serve with ice cream.

Serves 6

Chocolate and almond torte

150 g (5½ oz) flaked or whole
  almonds
1 slice pandoro sweet cake or 1 small
  brioche (about 40 g)
300 g (10½ oz) dark chocolate
2 tablespoons brandy
150 g (5½ oz) unsalted butter,
  softened
150 g (5½ oz) caster (superfine) sugar
4 eggs
1 teaspoon vanilla extract (optional)
200 g (7 oz) mascarpone cheese
cocoa powder, to dust
crème fraîche, to serve

Preheat the oven to 170°C (325°F/
Gas 4). Toast the almonds in the oven
for 8–10 minutes until golden brown.

Put the almonds and pandoro in a
food processor and process until the
mixture resembles breadcrumbs.
Grease a 23 cm (9 in) springform tin
with a little butter. Tip some of the
mixture into the tin and shake it
around so that it forms a coating on
the bottom and side of the tin. Put
the remaining nut mixture aside.

Gently melt the chocolate and brandy
in a heatproof bowl set over a
saucepan of simmering water, making
sure that the bowl does not touch
the water. Stir occasionally until the
chocolate has melted. Cool slightly.

Cream the butter and sugar in the
food processor or with a wooden
spoon for a few minutes until light and
pale. Add the melted chocolate, eggs,
vanilla and mascarpone. Add the
remaining nut mixture and mix well.
Tip into the tin.

Bake for 50–60 minutes, or until just
set. Leave to rest in the tin for about
15 minutes before taking out. Dust
with a little cocoa when cool and
serve with crème fraîche.

Venetian rice pudding

750 ml (3 cups) milk
250 ml (1 cup) thick (double/heavy)
  cream
1 vanilla pod, split
50 g (1³⁄₄ oz) caster (superfine) sugar
¼ teaspoon ground cinnamon
pinch grated nutmeg
1 tablespoon grated orange zest
85 g (3 oz) sultanas
2 tablespoons brandy or sweet
  Marsala
110 g (½ cup) risotto or pudding rice

Put the milk, double cream and vanilla pod in a heavy-based saucepan, and bring just to the boil, then remove from the heat. Add the sugar, cinnamon, nutmeg and orange zest, and set aside.

Put the sultanas and brandy in a small bowl and leave to soak. Add the rice to the infused milk and return to the heat. Bring to a simmer and stir slowly for 35 minutes, or until the rice is creamy. Stir in the sultanas and remove the vanilla pod at the end of cooking. Serve warm or cold.

Serves 4

Chocolate affogato

240 g (9 oz) dark chocolate
1 litre (4 cups) milk
6 eggs
110 g (½ cup) caster (superfine) sugar
340 ml (1⅓ cup) thick (double/heavy) cream
4 small cups of espresso or very strong coffee
4 shots Frangelico or any other liqueur that you like

Break the chocolate into individual squares and put it with the milk in a saucepan. Heat the milk over low heat — you must do this slowly or the chocolate will catch on the bottom. As the milk heats up and the chocolate melts, stir the mixture until you have a smooth liquid. You don't need to boil the milk, as the chocolate will melt at a much lower temperature. Whisk the eggs and sugar together with electric beaters, in a large glass or metal bowl, until the mixture is pale and frothy. Add the milk and chocolate mixture, along with the cream, and mix.

Pour the mixture into a shallow plastic or metal container and put it in the freezer. In order to make a smooth ice cream you will now have to whisk the mixture every hour or so to break up the ice crystals as they form. When the mixture gets very stiff, leave it to set overnight.

Scoop four balls of ice cream out of the container and put them into four cups, then put these in the freezer while you make the coffee.

Serve the ice cream with the Frangelico and coffee poured over it.

Serves 4

Basics

Boiling rice

Rinse the rice under cold running water until the water running away is clear, then drain well.

Put the rice in a heavy-based saucepan and add enough water to come about 5 cm (2 in) above the surface of the rice. Add 1 teaspoon of salt and bring the water quickly to the boil. When it boils, cover and reduce the heat to a simmer.

Cook for 15 minutes, or until the rice is just tender, then remove the saucepan from the heat and rest the rice for 10 minutes without removing the lid. Fluff the rice with a fork before serving.

Cooking noodles

Some noodles need to be softened in boiling water; others are cooked or fried, so always refer to the instructions on the packet. Cook noodles in plenty of boiling water and drain well.

If cooking small or individual portions of fresh noodles, put them in a sieve and dunk them in a saucepan of boiling water. This is a good method for quick-cooking noodles, such as egg noodles or rice noodles.

Cold noodles can be tossed in a little oil to keep them from sticking and then reheated in boiling water.

Cooking pasta

Pasta has to be cooked in lots of rapidly boiling salted water — about 1 litre (4 cups) of water and 1 teaspoon salt per 100 g (3½ oz) of pasta. The pan must be large enough for the pasta to move about freely.

It is not necessary to add oil to the cooking water or the draining pasta; all this does is coat the pasta and encourage the sauce to slide off.

When you drain pasta, don't do it too thoroughly — a little water left clinging to the pasta will help the sauce spread through it.

Pizza base

Mix 2 teaspoons dried yeast with 1 tablespoon sugar and 90 ml (⅓ cup) warm water and leave until the mixture bubbles.

Sift 450 g (1 lb) plain (all-purpose) flour into a bowl with a pinch of salt, add the yeast and 125 ml (½ cup) water and mix to a soft dough.

Knead the dough until smooth and springy — at least 5 minutes. Put in a bowl, cover and leave to rise until doubled in size.

Punch the air out of the dough with your fist and divide it into two equal pieces.

Flatten each piece of dough into a circle, then, working from the centre out, make the circle bigger using the heel of your hand.

Leave a slightly raised rim around the edge and place it on an oiled tray dusted with cornmeal. Add the topping.

Mashed potatoes

Peel and chop 4 large floury potatoes. Put them in cold water and bring them to the boil. Boil until tender, drain well and put them back in a saucepan over a low heat with 2 tablespoons of hot milk, 1 tablespoon of butter and plenty of seasoning.

Remove from the stove and mash with a masher, then beat with a wooden spoon until fluffy. If you like you can add more butter, a grating of nutmeg or a splash of cream. Serves 4.

Risotto

Use a large deep frying pan or shallow saucepan with a heavy base. Make sure the stock or liquid you are going to add is hot — keep it at a low simmer on the stove.

Cook the rice in the butter first. This creates a seal around the grains, trapping the starch. Stir frequently to prevent the rice from sticking to the bottom of the pan and to ensure all the grains are cooked evenly.

Add the liquid a ladleful at a time. Stir constantly. If you cook the rice too slowly, it will become gluey; too fast and the liquid will evaporate — keep it at a fast simmer.

Season the rice early on while it is absorbing flavour. Add just enough liquid to cover it so it cooks evenly. The rice should be *al dente*. Stop cooking the rice as soon as it is creamy but still has a little texture in the middle of the grain. The risotto should be rich and thick like porridge, not too wet or dry.

Chicken stock

Put 2 kg (4 lb 8 oz) chicken bones, trimmings, wings and necks in a large saucepan with 2 chopped carrots, 1 halved onion, 1 chopped leek,

1 chopped celery stalk, a bouquet garni and 6 peppercorns. Add 4 litres (16 cups) of cold water.

Bring to the boil and skim off any froth. Simmer the stock for 2 hours, skimming at regular intervals (adding a splash of cold water will precipitate any scum).

Strain the stock and leave to cool in the fridge. When it's cold, you can lift off the layer of fat from the top.

Vegetable stock

Put 500 g (1 lb 2 oz) mixed chopped carrots, celery, onions and leeks in a stockpot with a bouquet garni and 10 peppercorns.

Add 2.5 litres (10 cups) cold water and bring to the boil. Skim off any scum.

Simmer the stock for 1–2 hours, pressing the solids to extract all the flavour, then strain and cool in the fridge.

Fish stock

Put 2 kg (4 lb 8 oz) fish bones and heads, a bouquet garni, 1 chopped onion and 10 peppercorns in the pot.

Add 2.5 litres (10 cups) cold water and bring to the boil and simmer for 20–30 minutes. Skim off any scum.

Strain the stock, then cool in the fridge. When cool, lift off any congealed fat.

Pesto

Put 2 garlic cloves in a mortar and pestle or food processor, add a pinch of salt and 55 g (2 oz) pine nuts. Pound or whizz to a paste.

Gradually add 55 g (2 oz) basil leaves and pound or whizz the leaves into the base mixture. Stir in 70 g (2½ oz) grated Parmesan cheese, then gradually add 125 ml (½ cup) olive oil.

Use immediately or store covered in the fridge for up to 1 week. If storing, make sure the pesto surface is covered with a thin layer of olive oil. Makes 250 ml (1 cup).

Vinaigrette

Using a mortar and pestle, or the blade of a knife, crush 1 small garlic clove with a little salt to form a smooth paste. Add 1 tablespoon of good-quality vinegar and ½ teaspoon of Dijon mustard and mix well.

Gradually mix in 3 tablespoons of olive oil until a smooth emulsion is formed. Season with salt and pepper. Makes enough for one salad.

Melting chocolate

When melting chocolate, always use a clean, dry bowl. Water or moisture will make the chocolate seize (turn into a thick mass that won't melt), and overheating will make it scorch and taste bitter.

To melt chocolate, chop it into small even-sized pieces and place in a heatproof bowl. Bring a saucepan of water to the boil, then remove from the heat. Sit the bowl over the saucepan of water — make sure the bowl doesn't touch the water and that no water or steam gets into the bowl or the chocolate will seize. Leave the chocolate to soften a little, then stir until smooth and melted.

Remove the chocolate from the saucepan to cool, or leave in place over the hot water if you want to keep the chocolate liquid.

Meringue

To make one quantity of meringue, beat 6 egg whites and a pinch of cream of tartar in a clean, dry bowl with electric beaters until soft peaks form. Gradually pour in 340 g (1½ cups) caster (superfine) sugar, beating until the meringue is thick and glossy.

Whipping cream

Before whipping cream, chill the mixing bowl in the fridge.

For maximum volume, use a balloon whisk and beat well. You can use an electric whisk, but be careful you don't overbeat the cream and end up with butter.

Whisking egg whites

Eggs for whisking should be at room temperature as cold egg white will not whisk well. Always use a very clean and dry glass or metal bowl. Whisk the whites gently at first, then more vigorously until you reach the stage you want, ensuring you have beaten all the egg to the same degree.

At soft peak, the peaks on the egg white will flop; at stiff peak, only the very tops will flop. Egg whites, when properly whisked, will triple in volume.

Index

Index

Index

Photographers: Alan Benson, Cris Cordeiro, Craig Cranko, Ben Dearnley, Joe Filshie, Jared Fowler, Scott Hawkins, Ian Hofstetter, Chris L. Jones, Jason Lowe, Ashley Mackevicius, Andre Martin, Rob Reichenfeld, Brett Stevens.

Food Stylists: Kristen Anderson, Marie-Hélène Clauzon, Jane Collins, Carolyn Fienberg, Jane Hann, Mary Harris, Katy Holder, Cherise Koch, Sarah de Nardi, Michelle Noerianto, Sarah O'Brien, Sally Parker.

Food Preparation: Alison Adams, Shaun Arantz, Rekha Arnott, Jo Glynn, Sonia Grieg, Ross Dobson, Michelle Earle, Michelle Lawton, Michaela Le Compte, Valli Little, Olivia Lowndes, Kerrie Mullins, Briget Palmer, Kim Passenger, Justine Poole, Julie Ray, Christine Sheppard, Dimitra Stais, Angela Tregonning, and the Murdoch Books Test kitchen.

Published by Murdoch Books Pty Limited

Designer: Michelle Cutler (internals); Marylouise Brammer (cover)
Photographers: Jared Fowler (chapter openers); Stuart Scott (cover)
Stylists: Cherise Koch; (chapter openers); Louise Bickle (cover)
Editor: Gordana Trifunovic Production: Elizabeth Malcolm

Chief Executive: Juliet Rogers
Publishing Director: Kay Scarlett
Commissioning Editor: Lynn Lewis
Senior Designer: Heather Menzies

National Library of Australia Cataloguing-in-Publication Data
Title: Home food/editor, Lynn Lewis. ISBN 9781741964134 (pbk.)
Series: New chunky. Includes index. Subjects: Cookery. 641.5

Printed by 1010 Printing International Limited
PRINTED IN CHINA
First printed 2003. This edition 2009.

For fan-forced ovens, set the oven temperature to 20°C (35°F) lower than indicated in the recipe.
We have used 20 ml tablespoon measures. IMPORTANT: Those who might be at risk from the effects
of salmonella poisoning (the elderly, pregnant women, young children and those suffering from immune
deficiency diseases) should consult their GP with any concerns about eating raw eggs.

Cover credits: Heart print fabric, Spotlight. Green dinner plate, green and white ceramic entrée plates,
Dinosaur Designs. Duck egg strip dish and dipping bowl, pistachio square dish and pebble bowl,
Mud Australia. Marimekko Mini Unikko print fabric, Chee Soo & Fitzgerald. Ljungberg print fabric,
Roundabout. Floral print fabric, No Chintz. Front flap: Marimekko Mini Unikko print fabric,
Chee Soon & Fitzgerald.

A catalogue record for this book is available from the British Library.

Published by:
AUSTRALIA
Murdoch Books Pty Ltd
Pier 8/9, 23 Hickson Road,
Millers Point NSW 2000
Phone: + 61 (0) 2 8220 2000
Fax: + 61 (0) 2 8220 2558
www.murdochbooks.com.au

UK
Murdoch Books UK Ltd
Erico House, 6th Floor North,
93-99 Upper Richmond Rd,
Putney, London SW15 2TG
Phone: + 44 (0) 20 8785 5995
Fax: + 44 (0) 20 8785 5985
www.murdochbooks.co.uk